YORK MEDIEVAL TEXTS

General Editors

ELIZABETH SALTER & DEREK PEARSALL

TO MY WIFE

Ten Miracle Plays

Edited by

R. GEORGE THOMAS

Northwestern University Press
Evanston

SALEM COLLEGE LIBRARY
WINSTON-SALEM, N. C.

First published in the U.S.A. 1966 by
Northwestern University Press
under arrangement with Edward Arnold (Publishers) Ltd., London

Second Printing, 1968

822.1
T 366 T

Copyright © R. GEORGE THOMAS 1966

Printed in the United States of America

Library of Congress Catalog Card Number: 66–27881

General Preface

The present series of *York Medieval Texts* is designed for under-
graduates and, where the text is appropriate, for upper forms of
schools. Its aim is to provide editions of major pieces of Middle
English writing in a form which will make them accessible without
loss of historical authenticity. Texts are chosen because of their
importance and artistic merit, and individual volumes may contain a
single work, coherent extracts from a longer work, or representative
examples of a genre. The principle governing the presentation of the
text is to preserve the character of the English while eliminating
unnecessary encumbrances such as obsolete letters and manuscript
errors. Glossary and explanatory notes operate together to clarify the
text; special attention is paid to the interpretation of passages which
are syntactically rather than lexically difficult. The Introduction to each
volume, like the rest of the apparatus, is designed to set the work in
its proper literary context, and to provide the critical guidance most
helpful to present-day readers. The intention of the series is exclusively
literary: the Editors hope to attract a wider audience not only for
works within the accepted literary canon, but also for those which
have until now been regarded as 'specialist' in appeal, or which have
been presented as if they were.

This volume of selections from the *Miracle Plays* introduces readers
to medieval English drama, and in that sense can be regarded as a
useful primer for newcomers to the field. It is concerned not to over-
simplify, but to give an accurate impression of the wide range and the
individual excellences of the plays: it views them as parts of a medieval
pageant and as lively dramatic creations in their own right. All the
main cycles are represented in a series of ten plays which have not
been readily available in selections of Middle English texts: it is hoped
that they will suggest both the complexity and the unity of dramatic
experience provided by the complete cycles.

81038

Acknowledgements

I acknowledge my gratitude to the Trustees of the British Museum and the Huntington Library for their kind permission to print from manuscripts in their charge. Four of my colleagues at Cardiff have given me sustained help and support: Professor E. C. Llewellyn, Mr. Charles Elliott, Mr. Michael Quinn and Mr. W. O. Evans. The dedication of this book is an inadequate tribute to my wife who has assisted me at all points, and in so many ways, in the detailed preparation of the text and the glossary. Finally, I must thank the General Editors for their initial interest, informed criticism and helpful encouragement.

R. G. T.

Contents

Introduction

I. Early Development

With the fall of the Roman Empire, Roman Drama disappeared and most scholars assume that for the next five centuries or so any faint dramatic tradition that survived must have been passed on by the coarse and frequently indelicate Roman *mimes* to the medieval minstrels. Most recent scholars agree that, although the *mimes* went underground, they certainly kept alive a tradition of *acting* which, in essence, was ready to develop into *drama* when hostility to the act of imitation and representation had abated. For although the Church had many reasons for objecting to the drama of the late Roman period, the beginnings of modern drama were cradled and nurtured within the services of the Church, at first within the Mass and, later, in the freer atmosphere of Mattins.[1]

The best and most frequently illustrated example of a trope which proved capable of development into rudimentary imitation is the 'Quem quaeritis in sepulchro' trope[2] from the Mass for Easter Day which, when transferred to the office of Mattins for the same day, was acted by members of the choir even as

---

[1] For more detailed information see the following authorities:

E. K. Chambers, *The Medieval Stage*, vols. I and II (London, 1903). [Hereafter referred to as Chambers (*TMS*) I, II.]

Karl Young, *The Drama of the Medieval Church*, vols. I and II (Oxford, 1933). [Young I, II.]

E. K. Chambers, *English Literature at the Close of the Middle Ages* (Oxford, 1945). [Chambers (*CMA*).]

Hardin Craig, *English Religious Drama of the Middle Ages* (Oxford, 1960). [Craig.]

[2] A 'trope' was a verbal amplification of any passage used in the authorized liturgy of the Church. For example, at the end of the Mass a deacon announced the words *Ite, missa est*, to which the choir responded with *Deo gratias*. In one of the earliest recorded tropes from the ninth century an entire sentence was inserted between *Ite* and *missa* and *Deo* and *gratias;* such embellishments were developed musically and verbally during the Carolingian Renaissance and spread rapidly to all the key services of the Christian year. The most famous is the *quem-quaeritis* trope which belonged to the Introit of the Mass at Easter. The angels at the sepulchre ask the question, 'Whom do you seek in the sepulchre, O followers of Christ'; the Marys reply, 'Jesus of Nazareth who was crucified, O celestial beings', to which the angels respond further with 'He is not here; he is risen, exactly as he foretold. Go and proclaim that he has risen from the tomb.' These lines, based on *Mark* 16: 1–8, were sung as a dialogue-duet, and from this simple action the beginnings of medieval drama developed. Cf. Chambers (*TMS*) II, pp. 7–15 and 25–40; Young I, pp. 178–238; Craig, pp. 19–47; and *A Literary History of England*, ed. Kemp Malone and Albert C. Baugh, vol. I, *The Middle Ages* (New York, 1948), pp. 273–6

it was being chanted antiphonally. This trope is generally dated *c.* 900. Soon, similar dramatic developments took place at Christmas (e.g. connected with cribs and the shepherds) and on the Twelfth Day (i.e. the adoration of the Magi and the presentation of their gifts, and the Offices of the Star which appeared to them, the interview with Herod and the weeping of Rachel for her children). Another significant germ of dramatic development was the pseudo-Augustinian sermon 'Contra Judaeos, Paganos, et Arianos' which was often read at the Christmas Mattins. Gradually a long line of Old Testament prophets and worthies were introduced into this sermon in order to give point and force to the Old Testament testimony to the coming of Christ. Here was admirable material for processional speech and imitation which, in its later and more dramatic form, influenced the very structure of the Miracle Plays. Thus far, there is general agreement about the ecclesiastical and liturgical origins of the material which later developed into the medieval dramatic cycles. The accepted view is that the essential development of medieval religious drama took place between the tenth and the thirteenth centuries and that by the opening of the fourteenth century the most important themes of church drama had received full and characteristic treatment. Further, the numerous ecclesiastical strictures against drama were not directed against edifying dramatic performances but against the secular loutishness and ecclesiastical licence of the Feast of Fools and similar disorders which so humanly disrupted the liturgical year. Behind such strictures one can detect a desire not to avoid drama altogether but to encourage a return to the simpler representation which adorned the liturgy in the early Middle Ages.

II. *Later Developments*

No single picture of the next stage in the development of medieval drama commands general assent. There are three broad contentions as to when and why performances gradually 'broke their liturgical bonds'. First, the almost evolutionary view of growing, almost inevitable secularization. For instance, G. G. Coulton, believing that by the thirteenth century all drama was as far advanced as it could go within strictly religious limits, argues that 'up to this point we may treat them as "services" (*officia*); in their further development they have become "amusements" (*spectacula*)'.[3] This is the view commonly ascribed to E. K. Chambers—despite his many qualifications of it—of a process of gradual but increasing secularization from choir to nave, to churchyard, to market place, and, finally, to the theatre.[4] A. P. Rossiter carries this kind of argument much further: 'the simplest explanation of the "exit" from the church is that the secular world gave much more room for developments which were already pressing on inventive "literary" minds. The secular world

[3] G. G. Coulton, *Medieval Panorama* (Cambridge, 1938), p. 599
[4] Chambers (*CMA*), pp. 1–65

gave freedom and an impulse we may properly call artistic took the line of least resistance.'[5]

A second group of scholars deny that the plays were ever genuinely 'secularized' but that they remained, throughout the period of their effective growth, under the supervision of the church. By his re-examination of the Chester records, F. M. Salter has stood on end many earlier assumptions about the staging of the miracle plays and their official connection with the church. Stated briefly, his argument is that the only opposition to the plays came from the Church of England and that, as long as Roman influence endured in English life, the plays remained within its jurisdiction. At no time were they in secular hands but in the keeping of the abbeys and the guilds jointly, both of which institutions proved inadequate custodians.[6] This opinion has been vigorously supported by Glynne Wickham, the latest historian of the early English stage; he believes that new, original plays of the Fall, Crucifixion and Judgement were presented out of doors during the thirteenth century 'at the insistence of friars or like-minded priests and clerks' and that these plays attracted to themselves some of the techniques and materials from the worship of the church'.[7] This theory, with its inevitable reliance on the fruitful activities of the friars—those universal disseminators of new ideas and practices not only in the later Middle Ages, but also in all modern theories about this period—seems to draw quite legitimately on the researches of G. R. Owst[8] into preaching in late medieval times.

A third and intermediate view, to which in some measure and on certain points both sides seem to subscribe, is that held by Karl Young and Hardin Craig. Young accepts the validity of the view that the transfer from ecclesiastical to secular auspices was effected 'through the desire of both playwrights and audience for an increase in the scope of the performance, for an enrichment of context and for the use of the vernacular'.[9] It is this last point which most attracts Craig and which to me is the nub of the whole later development and literary appeal of the English Miracle Plays. Craig cautions one against laying too much stress on the Latin plays (which are so much more widely preserved on the Continent than in England) as the immediate sources for the miracle plays.[10] His contention is that the Latin plays were not literary sources in the

[5] A. P. Rossiter, *English Drama from Early Times to the Elizabethans*, Hutchinson's University Library (London, 1950), p. 50

[6] F. M. Salter, *Medieval Drama in Chester* (London, 1955), pp. 54–80 and pp. 40–5

[7] Glynne Wickham, *Early English Stages 1300 to 1660*, vol. I, 1300–1576 (London, 1959), p. 316

[8] G. R. Owst, *Literature and Pulpit in Medieval England* (Cambridge, 1933)

[9] Young II, p. 42 and, more generally, pp. 397–426

[10] Craig, pp. 18, 88–114, 143–57. Young II, pp. 307–60, supplies in full the texts of the Latin plays of St Nicholas that have been preserved. They reflect

modern sense; they passed on to the mystery stages 'through some vernacular channel'.[11] He observes that 'the greatest body of Middle English literature is devoted to the presentation in English poetry or prose of the great mass of medieval Latin religious literature'.[11] Drawing attention to the comedy, coarseness and vulgarity which abound in the apocryphal literature of the late Middle Ages, he notes that these works are essentially religious in origin; he seems to imply that the presence of these same qualities in the plays is no guarantee of the absence of ecclesiastical purpose. Like Young, Craig seems poised between the two sides with a tendency to ascribe and relate the later development of the English plays to native English conditions.

This is no open and shut case. One fact is incontrovertible though: about the end of the fourteenth century, an elaborate Wycliffite *Treatise of Miraclis Pleyinge*[12] condemned what were obviously popular dramatic performances.

Thereafter evidence accumulates for the existence of plays in the vernacular, but the sequence of events will remain unclear until some theory explains why the scattered Latin liturgical dramas appeared, some two centuries later, as the great mystery cycles.[13] All historians of the drama agree that there is some close connection between the cycles of plays that we now know (from the fifteenth and sixteenth century manuscript collections) and the institution of Corpus Christi day which was observed in England from 1318 onwards. Many Corpus Christi Guilds were founded and, in varying degrees, the performance of

---

the period from the early thirteenth to the early fourteenth century when the plays were presumably still in the hands of the clergy, and illustrate quite clearly the growing use of the vernacular languages in Germany, France and England. The range of the Latin plays can also be studied in *Chief Pre-Shakespearean Dramas*, ed. J. Q. Adams (New York, 1924), pp. 51–69 and, for the introduction of the vernacular into the Shrewsbury fragments, pp. 73–8

[11] Craig, p. 157

[12] *Reliquiae Antiquae*, vol. II, p. 42; quoted in Chambers (*EMS*) II, p. 102

[13] The cycles of mystery plays seem to have been a feature of the larger towns, and there is evidence for their existence in about twelve places in England, especially York (*York Plays*), Wakefield (*Towneley Plays*), Chester (*Chester Plays*), Coventry (*Two Coventry Corpus Christi Plays*), Beverley, Newcastle-upon-Tyne, Norwich, Worcester. The *Ludus Coventriae* (sometimes referred to as *Hegge Plays*) were wrongly identified with Coventry but the Proclamation, which advertises its performance, states that it will be given in 'N. towne', where 'N' probably stands for the Latin word *nomen*, which suggests that the name of the appropriate town was substituted for 'N'. There are also two plays about *Abraham and Isaac* and a complete cycle of plays in the Cornish language, comprising a play about the Creation (and the Fall of Lucifer), a series of O.T. plays, a Passion Play, and a drama on the Resurrection and Ascension. (For the chief editions of the English Cycles see the *Select Bibliography*, p.15.)

Miracle Plays was attached to this feast; furthermore, 'Corpus Christi plays' can be traced in widely different parts of Britain. W. W. Greg states the case for the connection between the feast and the plays: 'It seems to me more reasonable [that is, than that processional drama actually sprang from the Corpus Christi procession] to suppose that previously existing plays somehow became attached to the procession, or that new ones were written on existing models to suit a new method of representation.'[14] Clearly, then, the Miracle Plays dealt with in this selection can be traced in their early vernacular form and general shape, as far back as the second quarter of the fourteenth century. Wickham would go further; he sees 'no reason to doubt that laymen, banded into representative professional groups, were invited to participate in the great procession', and believed that 'in the latter part of the fourteenth century, laymen were already associated with particular scenes and stories'. He suggests that, then, 'with ecclesiastical permission, they could even appropriate the plays'.[15]

To harmonize these conflicting views in the present state of our knowledge is impossible. The problem is intrinsically simple of statement and inordinately difficult of solution. How did English medieval drama develop into the Miracle Plays which are so radically different in spirit, if not in purpose, from the Latin religious drama? There are many red herrings across this trail. How many large cycles can we presume to be lost? Were the plays of the North so radically different from the 'passion plays' of the South? Will a recent study on Lollardy in the diocese of York alter the older view of a conservative Catholic North of England clinging to old customs and incidentally preserving them for the benefit (and confusion) of scholars?[16] What is the relationship of these plays to the Morality Plays, the Tudor Interludes,[17] or to Elizabethan Drama? How best to explain this strong Northern development of the vernacular in a century that is not normally regarded as favourable to new literary endeavours? The greatest stumbling-block of all is that which divides those who wish to attribute all that is best in late medieval literature to the consciously fostering hand of Mother Church from those who deny Holy Church anything but a villain's part. Whichever of these two latter views is taken will inevitably colour one's whole perspective of what is good and what is of permanent value in the plays that have come down to us.

This present selection has been prepared under the influence of what I believe to be the best inspiration of both sides. It represents deliberately the grand

---

[14] W. W. Greg, *Bibliographical and Textual Problems of the English Miracle Cycles* (London, 1914), p. 19

[15] *Op. cit.*, p. 149; see also pp. 120–8, 145–9, 262–6, 272–3

[16] A. G. Dickens, *Lollards and Protestants in the Diocese of York 1509–1558* (London, 1959)

[17] Cf. T. W. Craik, *The Tudor Interlude: Stage, Costume, and Acting* (Leicester, 1961)

medieval conception of Man's Fall, Christ's Redemption and the Judgement Day which, it seems to me, was as relevant to Chaucer's thinking as it was to Marlowe's dramaturgy. Thus much of common belief Lollard and Pardoner, Friar and Poor Parson would accept. What the Wakefield Master[18] and other unknown makers added to this belief was a reflection of that intense, growing awareness of nationhood and of the untapped resources of the mother-tongue which has been a source of recurring joy and pleasure to every reader of the many collections of medieval English manuscripts. The power of this common belief to attract assent may have diminished for twentieth century readers, but it would be an act of critical folly to praise the forceful idiom of the playwrights as merely an adventitious embellishment on an unacceptable theme. For our interest in the living quality of these vernacular plays will depend ultimately on the ability of their authors to match the utmost resources of the spoken and written language to the greatest theme that they could believe in or intuitively comprehend.

III. *A Question of Names*

The choice of the most appropriate name for the plays included in this selection could be a matter for considerable discussion and dispute. There are three possible terms: 'miracle play', 'mystery play', and 'morality' (play). Since the dramatic remains are so much more numerous and varied on the Continent than they are in England, some scholars have turned to continental terminology in order to clarify the problem. I think it wise to keep the term 'Morality (Play)' for those plays which clearly derive from the Dance of Death and which merged imperceptibly into the Tudor Interludes. The earliest play of this type (*The Pride of Life*) dates from *c.* 1400 and its most famous examples, *The Castle of Perseverance, Mind, Will and Understanding,* and *Everyman* belong to the second half of the fifteenth century. The term 'Morality' then can be usefully retained and distinguished for this later kind of play. A few scholars would prefer to call the great English collections (of York, Towneley, Chester and 'Coventry') 'cycles of mystery plays'. This is an attractive solution if only because the word 'mystery' can still somehow be equated with the craft of a guild and, in the form that we now have them, all these surviving plays—and the records that point to them—suggest a close connection with the craft guilds. I notice that although at one point early in his study Dr Wickham writes that unfortunately 'medieval drama is thought of exclusively in terms of Mystery and Morality Plays',[19] elsewhere he refers to our kind of play as a 'Miracle Play'. The objections to the term 'mystery' are many and the distinction between *mystery* and *miracle* in the context of European (and particularly

[18] His work and personality are most conveniently presented in '*The Wakefield Pageants in the Towneley Cycle*, ed. A. C. Cawley (Manchester, 1958).
[19] Wickham, *op. cit.,* p. 3

French) literature is well argued by Hardin Craig. The distinction between the two terms seems to be relevant to English drama in the pre-vernacular period. For example, Craig uses the word 'mystery' to 'designate that group of religious plays of the Middle Ages that are based ultimately on Scripture and arose from the service in the cursus of the liturgical year', and the word 'miracle' to 'denote those that treat of the lives and martyrdom of the saints'.[20] I have followed E. K. Chambers: 'I think it is an illegitimate transference to English usage of a distinction between hagiological *miracles* and biblical *mystères*, which was made in French terminology from the end of the fourteenth century onwards. No English play was, however, called a "mystery" before 1744. . . . I feel little doubt myself that the normal English term was "miracle" . . . covering all out-of-door vernacular religious plays.'[21] The term was tough enough to be used in Latinized form, and the title of the Wycliffite treatise, to say nothing of the example of most English writers on the subject, seems to clinch the choice of *Miracle Play*.

IV. *Acting and Actors*

The alleged 'bareness' and 'crudity' of the performances of these Miracle Plays have lately been vigorously challenged. Salter[22] pours doubt on the validity of all earlier interpretations of the Chester records in supporting this view. Southern's analysis[23] of *The Castle of Perseverance* (c. 1425) reveals a colourful, fast-moving performance which combined pageantry, poetry, music and *drama*. Wickham's wider survey of the development of a variety of indoor and open-air entertainments in the Middle Ages lends strong support to the opinions of the other two, as well as offering a new interpretation of the special nature of the processional performances at Chester as recorded by David Rogers[24] in the sixteenth century. All three agree with the opinion expressed by H. C. Gardiner in *Mysteries' End*[25] that the 'demise of the plays' was not due to the difficulties of the Guilds in putting on these new and increasingly elaborate productions but to the 'hostility of the new Church'. In other words, the Elizabethan dramatists did not have to begin *de novo;* they could draw on a richer dramatic heritage than was at one time thought possible.

Salter's researches into the history, cost and maintenance of the Chester pageant houses point to 'stages that were sizeable, with ample floor space for elaborate spectacles'.[26] Acoustics, and the need to use intricate machinery for

---

[20] Craig, pp. 320–3, 341–3   [21] Chambers (*CMA*), pp. 15, 16
[22] *Op. cit.*, pp. 81–4
[23] R. Southern, *The Medieval Theatre in the Round* (London, 1957)
[24] *Harley MS* 1944, fol. 21. Quoted by Salter, *op. cit.*, p. 55
[25] H. C. Gardiner, *Mysteries' End, an Investigation of the Last Days of the Medieval Religious Stage* (New Haven: Yale U.P., 1946)
[26] *Op. cit.*, p. 64 and, more generally, pp. 62–9

ascents and descents, presuppose a strong roof, which leaves Rogers' 'open roof' quite unacceptable. Again, for a slightly earlier period, Southern shows the mechanics of an 'unlocalized' stage situated in the centre of a permanent amphitheatre, with tiers for the spectators and fixed scaffolds for 'mansions' distributed around the acting 'place' to safeguard the sight-lines of viewers. Wickham suggests that, at least in Chester, the stage was in two movable parts, each with its own waggon: one contained the fixed sets (the mansions), the machinery, and a tiring house, while the other provided an extra apron stage to give the traditional 'place' or acting area. The spectators would be accommodated in the houses which flanked the narrow streets as they did for other processions of a civic and ceremonial character. Taken together, all this reconstruction appears to be more practicable than previous suggestions.

It is not so easy to demonstrate the continuity of an acting tradition which, I believe, must have been sufficiently sophisticated to support the claims which are now being made for the high standard of performance attained by the late Miracle Plays. Because of the continued hostility of the ecclesiastical authorities to the profession of *histrio* until the early fourteenth century, we must assume that, even while the earlier liturgical and religious drama was developing in the hands of amateur ecclesiastical playwrights and actors, the professional actor— descendant of Roman *mimes*, Northern *scop* and Romance *trouvère*— found his natural outlet and livelihood in a minstrel troupe (under the protection of a powerful patron) which gave performances of a varied nature on festive occasions. He had to be versatile, combining the skill of 'dancer, acrobat, musician, reciter of gestes, juggler or clown'. Dr Wickham believes that by the mid-fifteenth century the familiar Tudor separation of functions (into player, musician, fool or jester) was in process of taking place. As a gloss on this broader picture we may note Salter's insistence that the Chester records of payment imply that a few of the actors there were paid at rates which suggest professional skill. Southern's account of his theatre in the round almost presupposes, it seems to me, a small mobile professional company.

Clearly, then, the professional troupes toured the principal Fairs and took advantage of the opportunities afforded by Saints' Days for finding a ready audience. And if, in the later Middle Ages, Miracle Plays were also performed on such occasions, there must have been considerable interaction between the two kinds of entertainment. The recent assumption is that, although the ecclesiastical authorities maintained control over the scripts of the Miracle Plays and finally decided the dates on which they were to be performed, the Guilds, who were naturally concerned with the production of the plays, would be more likely to draw on the experience of the professionals. One safeguard is necessary, I think, amid all this careful yet speculative reconstruction: conditions in Chester or Coventry must not be raised to the level of a general rule for all Miracle Plays everywhere in England. It is enough to use recent scholarship to demonstrate that the productions of the plays were as admirably matched to the sublimity of their theme as money, good will, mechanical ingenuity, pious intent and histrionic ability could make them.

Finally, the part played by music in these performances must not be over-looked by a too narrow concentration on the texts themselves.[27] R. W. Ingram has reminded us that 'music, the simplest and most popular pastime in medieval society, was an important addition to the entertainment of the plays'.[28] The possibilities of music were not explored all at once, but even the Chester Cycle—presumably the earliest—shows an admixture of Latin hymns (derived from the earlier liturgical performances) and vernacular songs. The most complete fusion of music into the action can be found in the Coventry Pageants, and the records of that town give some idea of the musical resources that could be drawn upon for these productions and the great care that was taken in the provision of songs. While it would be injudicious at present to interpret the evidence of the use of music to support either the 'secular' or the 'ecclesiastical' theory of the later development of the vernacular Miracle Plays, the modern reader should add the splendour of anthem singing, the virtuosity of a skilled instrumentalist, and the purity of boys' voices to the final effect of some of the great dramatic moments in these plays. To this extent musicologists and stage historians agree: these performances were not crude dialect representations made by ill-rehearsed amateurs on a bare stage surrounded by the laughable disguises of angels' wings, hell's mouth, and the rest. In the last resort attendance at these plays could be an act of the whole man, occasionally, at least, bridging the yawning gap between the real and the ideal which for many of us has become the hall-mark of so many late medieval institutions and beliefs.

V. *The Present Selection*

In making the present selection, the editor had two principles in mind: first, to give the reader some idea of the range and scope of the subjects which were tackled in a cycle of plays, and secondly, to provide texts of plays that are not readily available in selections of Middle English texts. Wherever possible the text for this edition has been prepared from the manuscripts; contractions have been silently expanded and modern punctuation introduced. Otherwise the text of the ten Miracle Plays is exactly as found in the manuscript selected for each play. Wherever possible the entire play is printed, but in a few instances con-siderations of space have made a few cuts necessary: these are indicated in the head-note to each play.

This present selection has also been compiled with the following additional

[27] Wickham, *op. cit.*, p. 176
[28] R. W. Ingram, 'The Use of Music in the English Miracle Plays', *Anglia*, lxxv (1957), 55–76

aims. First, to indicate the range of subjects and attitudes that were experienced by attendance at any performance of a complete cycle of miracle plays; secondly, by the selection of individual manuscripts written down at different times, to suggest the complexity of dramatic experiences that must necessarily lie behind any use of the term 'miracle play'; and, thirdly, to offer the reader a sufficiently varied sample of run-of-the-mill pageants to enable him to comprehend some of the assumptions of a late medieval audience, and, through the subsequent reading of the complete cycles of plays, to arrive at a juster appreciation of their true quality as a body of oral drama born out of the needs, aspirations and tensions of an entire community.

The phrase 'grand design of the miracle plays' may sound pretentious, but some such uniform conception certainly exists behind the York, Towneley, Chester and 'Coventry' Plays. A modern reader, living in a secular society, has to break down many barriers of assumption before he is able to accept the harmonious blend of exegesis, didacticism and histrionic skill which characterizes these pageants. This is no easy Rubicon to cross—particularly in view of the splendid flowering of Elizabethan drama. The 'grand design' challenges our most cherished assumptions about the place (and nature) of entertainment in our own lives; even more significantly, it challenges our conception of the function of religion in contemporary society and entertainment. Admittedly, there has been a revival of interest in 'religious drama' in England during the last thirty years, but the movement has not found a permanent place in the popular theatre, and the audience for religious plays, one suspects, has been drawn largely from church-goers who attend a 'good cause', just a shade more intellectual and worthy of support than attendance at a fête or a bazaar. On the twentieth-century English stage, the plays of T. S. Eliot, Christopher Fry and Ronald Duncan—their own intrinsic merits apart—are phenomena distinguished by their difference from the ordinary run of theatrical successes. They seem to have contributed little to the dramatic experience of the average theatre-goer or the spectator of cinematic or television performances. I am suggesting that these latter experiences of drama are the ones which a modern reader is most likely to bring to the miracle plays. Against such a norm, the pageants in this selection are very odd indeed.

The miracle plays seem to have provided popular entertainment for at least 150 years, and probably for a longer period. To be so successful, didactic plays need to be closely identified with the aspirations of the community that produces them. (And in a literal sense—despite the evidence that points to some employment of professional actors—community groups were responsible for their dramatic production.) From time to time, our own society has given rise to situations in which didactic dramatic entertainment has proved as acceptable to certain limited audiences as the pageants were to entire late-medieval communities. War-time films begged many questions of right and wrong in the interest of patriotic cohesion; the plays and revues of the English Left Wing movement in the 1930s (e.g. those by Auden and Isherwood) were riotously received by faithful party members in London and the provinces; and, more recently in the 1950s, the original 'anti-establishment' vogue centred around the Royal Court Theatre was born out of the demands of a generation of theatre-goers who had failed to find satisfactory entertainment in the commercial theatre of the West End. Even so, such examples of 'drama with a purpose' reflect the fissiparous nature of a secular, democratic community. Though the miracle plays were not the only form of entertainment in their day, their widespread and long-continued success suggests that they gave adequate dramatic expression to the cultural needs of an entire community. There are good reasons for their adequacy. Behind the grand design of man's fall, redemption and final judgement lay the ready acceptance of the Church's teaching by dramatist, actor and spectator. Despite many of the dramatists' evident enjoyment of the crudities, comedy, and quirks of fallen human nature, the credal statements that constitute the backbone of each cycle reveal a shared belief in the grand design as an acceptable intellectual formulation of man's place in the universe and of the necessary relationship that existed between his time spent on this earth and the time-span of eternity. The time-scale implicit in the grand design itself assisted the spectator in accepting the accuracy of the intellectual formulation on which it was based; in addition, his conditioned, unquestioning acceptance (from earliest childhood) of its revealed truth was a powerful aid towards the willing suspension of disbelief. For example, the three-tiered stage—with Hell below, Heaven above, and Earth as the principal playing-area—may appear crude to us although we can see the necessary force of the convention as an active one on the Elizabethan stage. One could argue that this particular convention was but a device to Marlowe's audience and that it would have appeared technically unconvincing to all but the merest bumpkins around the playing areas of York, Chester, and Wakefield. Such an opinion is itself the product of too crude a view of the nature of dramatic illusion in any theatre at any time and a denial of the many delicately graded adjustments and responses that we are still capable of making once our interest is engaged in the threate, at the opera, or before the screen. (Was it the 'cold', 'rational' eighteenth-century England that gave rise to Handel's *The Messiah*?) But to the original spectators the three-tier stage was neither a mere convention nor a convenient symbolic device as neutral as, say, the co-ordinates of a map reference. All their choices, the essence of their moral experience, confirmed the rightness of this grand design as a necessary and sufficient condition for understanding the pilgrim's progress from the cradle to the grave—and beyond it.

The plain truth is, then, that our present-day experience of plays comparable to the miracle plays is quite inadequate. Naïvely one thinks of Christmas plays at school, of tourist visits to Oberammergau, or of village pageants to celebrate

SALEM COLLEGE LIBRARY
WINSTON-SALEM, N. C.

the Festival of Britain or a Coronation. Such comparisons seem incomplete because they lack the vital wholeness of context within which the pageants were enacted. The frame of mind of the spectator at Wakefield (or N-town) was not one of solely intellectual assent, or of participation in a ritual ceremony, or of tolerant amusement before light, if socially accepted entertainment suitable for a major Feast. Nor, I suggest, was his reaction to the pageants the outcome of a nicely balanced embracing of all three attitudes. Rather, the pageants were a confirmation—through the media of speech, action, song and spectacle—of the living faith and powerful assumptions of an entire community which believed itself to be an integral part of a wider community (or *ecclesia*) which encompassed all space and all time, and of which all spectators had some experience through the acts of worship, confession and communion which were as natural as breathing to the experience of medieval men.

Within the framework of this larger, unshakeable area of stability, the anonymous dramatists and actors found unrivalled opportunities for histrionic skill, realistic imitation and traditional exposition. Probably, the least profitable approach to the 'grand design' is the evolutionary one: that is, to assume that the miracle plays formed but one stage in the development of some platonically conceived 'ideal drama' which reached its fulfilment in the plays of Shakespeare. There isn't enough evidence, nor, indeed, are there sufficient extant plays, to enable any such general statement to be made with confidence about 'the history of medieval English drama'. Nor is it at all possible to carry in one's mind a simple paradigm of what a miracle play was and how it was performed. The conflicting theories on such points have already been given above; their very conflict is a bar to the acceptance of any hold-all theory. In this selection I have resisted the temptation to include any plays which are confidently attributed to the 'Wakefield Master' as samples of what the pageants could become at their dramatic best.[29] I have come to see how untypical his plays were—not only of the other extant miracle plays, but also of the staple dramatic experience for which all the cycles seemed to provide. Consequently, plays have here been selected from all periods of composition (including the fair copy made at York and the late Chester copy of 1603) in order to illustrate the length of the time-span of the pageants' vital performance and the many and varied kinds of dramatic activity that are included under this general blanket term of 'miracle play'. Curiously enough, despite the different degrees of dramatic skill revealed by these ten pageants, certain common features emerge. Foremost is the skeletal framework of Scriptural (and Apocryphal) reference; next is the successful exploitation of the notion of an unlocalized playing area with its ready access to Heaven and (later) to Hell; thirdly, there is the constant cross-reference between the plays, which is inevitable because of the common

[29] See Cawley's excellent edition (*op. cit.*). *The Killing of Abel* is attributed only in part to this much-loved dramatist.

core of scriptural and exegetical tradition. Lastly, but constantly, there is the inclusion of the audience in the action by direct address and, even more, by the comic by-play which exploits the vernacular idiom, cuts across the stilted verse-pattern, and satisfies the spectator's basic demand for complete involvement in the performance he is watching.

An understanding of the approach to comedy in these pageants can bring the present-day reader a little closer to the purpose (and possibly to the cause of the success) of all the miracle plays. The premiss for all their comic characters was the acceptance of man's fallen nature and the blind pride of devils. Comedy develops from within the pattern of obedience to God's will (on which medieval society was theoretically based) which would inevitably result in a life of virtue and which was the accepted (if rarely attained) norm of ideal Christian conduct. The demonstration of such obedience can serve many purposes in the plays: it is the yardstick by which the conduct of all characters was judged and by which the rare, blessed characters could be recognized. Such obedience distinguishes Abel, Noah, Abraham, Balaam, David, the Blessed Virgin Mary, and Christ himself. The 'popular' characters in all cycles were the characters who disobeyed and thus shared with us all the ordinary human weaknesses: they, too, are the targets for laughter, coarseness, blasphemy, 'realism', and humour. Viewed in this way, Cain, Herod, the young adulterer escaping with his breeches down, the dicers at the foot of the Cross and the devils at the Harrowing of Hell, all share one quality with the spectator: their disobedience to God's commands and, its obverse, their hope (or despair) of receiving His grace and favour. The humour of the pageants is a product of the beliefs of the community that produced them.

In this context 'wit' is unnecessary and unattainable. Wit is an expression of the detached observer who prizes the intellectual awareness of separateness and nice distinctions. (Irony is more possible because it implies the forceful confrontation of two contrasting standards of judgement.) The dramatic experience of the miracle plays, I believe, was one of confirmation and acceptance: it gave proof of one's identity with one's fellows, with the society in which one lived, and with the common faith that supported all men within that society.[30] The salve of humour—however coarse, blasphemous, or sadistic it appears to the present-day reader—was born out of this sense of community shared by spectators and performers. Like the amusing asides of some famous Welsh nonconformist preachers, or C. H. Spurgeon's many illustrative anecdotes, or Chaucer's Pardoner's inset tale, the presence of humour or relief in the middle of serious exposition helps to sweeten the moral pill as it widens the terms of reference within which the theological argument is conducted. Abstract de-

[30] It is significant that many of the comic, non-accepting characters swear by 'Mahound', who stands for the Mohammedan threat to Christian unity and to its superiority as a creed.

monstration gains from concrete illustration. In addition, the comic scenes brought the gospel up to date by bridging the chronological gap between Then and Now. The grand design of the Miracle Plays began at one fixed point and would end at Doomsday; the various dramatic presentations of that design were conceived in living, contemporary terms with the continuous present as their appropriate verbal tense: 'time held them, green and dying', though at times they 'sang in their chains like the sea'.

Select Bibliography

1. Sources

York Mystery Plays, ed. L. Toulmin-Smith (Oxford, 1885)

The Chester Plays, ed. H. Deimling, *E.E.T.S.* (Extra Series), 62 (London, 1892, 1916, 1959)

The Towneley Plays, ed. G. England and A. W. Pollard, *E.E.T.S.* (Extra Series), 71 (London, 1897)

Specimens of Pre-Shakespearean Drama, ed. J. M. Manly, 2 vols. (New York, 1897)

Two Coventry Corpus Christi Plays, ed. H. Craig, *E.E.T.S.* (Extra Series), 87 (London, 1902, 1957)

Ludus Coventriae, ed. K. S. Block, *E.E.T.S.* (Extra Series), 120 (London, 1922, 1960)

Chief Pre-Shakespearean Dramas, ed. J. Q. Adams (New York, 1924)

English Miracle Plays, Moralities and Interludes, ed. A. W. Pollard (Oxford, 1927)

The York Cycle of Mystery Plays: A complete version, adapted by J. S. Purvis (London, 1957)

The Wakefield Pageants in the Towneley Cycle, ed. A. C. Cawley (Manchester, 1958). [See its bibliography, pp. xxxiv–xxxviii.]

The Chester Mystery Plays, adapted into Modern English by M. Hussey (London, 1958)

2. History and Criticism

M. D. Anderson, *Drama and Imagery in English Medieval Churches* (Cambridge, 1963)

P. F. Baum, 'The Medieval Legend of Judas Iscariot', *P.M.L.A.*, xxxi (1916), 481–632

John E. Bernbrock, 'Notes on the Towneley Cycle Slaying of Abel', *J.E.G.P.*, lxii (1963), 317–22

Arthur Brown, 'Some notes on Medieval Drama in York', in *Early English and Norse Studies Presented to Hugh Smith* (London, 1963)

E. Martin Browne, 'Producing the Mystery Plays Modern Audiences', *Drama Survey* III (Minneapolis, 1963), 5–15

E. K. Chambers, *The Medieval Stage*, 2 vols. (London, 1903)
  English Literature at the close of the Middle Ages (Oxford, 1945)

Hardin Craig, *English Religious Drama of the Middle Ages* (Oxford, 1960)

T. W. Craik, *The Tudor Interlude: Stage, Costume, and Acting* (Leicester, 1961)

H. C. Gardiner, *Mysteries' End, an Investigation of the Last Days of the Medieval Religious Stage* (New Haven, 1946)

W. W. Greg, *Bibliographical and Textual Problems of the English Miracle Cycles* (London, 1914)

R. W. Ingram, 'The Use of Music in the English Miracle Plays', *Anglia*, lxxv (1957), 55–76

E. Prosser, *Drama and Religion in the English Mystery Plays: A Re-evaluation* (Stanford, 1961)

J. W. Robinson, 'The Art of the York Realist', *M. P.*, lx (1963), 241–51

A. P. Rossiter, *English Drama from Early Times to the Elizabethans* (London, 1950)

F. M. Salter, *Medieval Drama in Chester* (London, 1955)

R. Southern, *The Medieval Theatre in the Round* (London, 1957)

Carl J. Stratman, *Bibliography of Medieval Drama* (Berkeley and Los Angeles, 1954)

Glynne Wickham, *Early English Stages, 1300 to 1660*, vol. I, 1300–1576 (London, 1959)

Arnold Williams, *The Drama of Medieval England* (Michigan, 1961)

Karl Young, *The Drama of the Medieval Church*, 2 vols. (Oxford, 1933)

I. The Proclamation

The Proclamation, which precedes the first play (about *The Creation of Heaven and the Angels*) in the *Ludus Coventriae*, is an integral part of the extant manuscript. This suggests the semi-official support given to the Miracle Plays. *The Proclamation*—of which only a sample is printed here—raises its own problems about the total number of plays in this particular group and about the place where these plays were originally performed. It ends with these words spoken by the third herald:

> At vi of the belle we gynne oure play
> In N. town, wherfore we pray
> That God now be youre spede. Amen.

In all, forty-one pageants were announced by the three heralds. The manuscript is attributed to the third quarter of the fifteenth century; its dialect is a Northern one, but some revisions suggest an attempt to remove archaic or dialectal forms by later users of the manuscript.

MS: British Museum, Cotton Vespasian D. VIII.

1ST HERALD	Now gracyous God, groundyd of all goodnesse,
	As thi grete glorie nevyr be-gynning had
	So thou socour and save all tho that sytt and sese
	And lystenyth to oure talkyng, with sylens stylle and sad.

    5 For we purpose us pertly stylle in this prese
       The pepyl to plese with pleys ful glad;
       Now lystenyth us lovely, bothe more and lesse.
       Gentyllys and yemanry of goodly lyf lad this tyde,
       We shall you shewe, as that we kan,
  10 How that this werd fyrst be-gan
       And how God made bothe molde and man,
       If that ye wyl abyde.

2ND HERALD   In the fyrst pagent we thenke to play
       How God dede make, thurowe his owyn myth,
  15 Hevyn so clere upon the fyrst day
       And ther-in he sett angell ful bryth.

5-6. For we intend, publicly before this very crowd, to entertain the public with plays.

　　　　Than angell with songe, this is no nay,
　　　　Shal worchep God as it is ryth;
　　　　But Lucifer, that angell so gay,
20　　In suche pompe than is he pyth
　　　　And set in so gret pride,
　　　　That Goddys sete he gynnyth to take,
　　　　Hese Lordys pere hymself to make;
　　　　But than he fallyth, a fend ful blake,
25　　From hevyn in helle to abyde.

3RD HERALD　　In the secund pagent, by Godys myth,
　　　　We thenke to shewe and pley be-dene
　　　　In the other sex days; by opyn syth
　　　　What thenge was wrought ther shal be sene.
30　　How best was made and foule of flyth
　　　　And last was man made, as I wene;
　　　　Of mannys o ryb, as I yow plyth,
　　　　Was woman wrought, mannys make to bene,
　　　　And put in paradyse.
35　　Ther were flourys bothe blew and blake;
　　　　Of all frutys thei myth ther take,
　　　　Saff frute of cunnyng thei shulde for-sake
　　　　And towche it no wyse.

　　　　The serpent toke Eve an appyl to byte
40　　And Eve toke Adam a mursel of the same;
　　　　Whan thei had do thus a-gens the rewle of ryte,
　　　　Than was oure Lord wroth and grevyd al with
　　　　　　grame.
　　　　Oure Lord gan appose them, of ther gret delyte,
　　　　Both to askuse hem of that synful blame;
45　　And than almythy God, for that gret dyspite,
　　　　Assygned hem grevous peyn, as ye shal se in game
　　　　In dede.
　　　　Seraphyn, an angell gay,
　　　　With brennyng swerd, this is verray,

17-18. Then (when He had done this), believe me, the angels would be able
to sing fitting praise to God.

43-4. Our Lord, because of their great joy, challenged them both to give
reasons that would excuse their sinful error.

50 From paradise bete hem a-way,
   In Bybyl as we rede.

1ST HERALD   We purpose to shewe, in the thryd pagent,
   The story of Caym, and of hese brother Abelle;
   Of here tythyngys, now be we bent,
55 In this pagent the trewth to telle:
   How the tythyng of Abel with feyr was brent
   And accept to God, yf ye wyl dwelle,
   We purpose to shewe, as we have ment,
   And how he was kyllyd of his brother so felle.
60 And than,
   How Caym was cursyd in al degre
   Of Godys owyn mowthe, ther shal ye se;
   Of trewe tythyng this may wel be
   Exawple to every man.

2ND HERALD 65 The iij^{de} pagent is now yow tolde.
   The fourte pagent of Noe shal be—
   How God was wroth with man on molde.
   Because fro synne man dede not fle,
   He sent to Noe an angel bolde
70 A shyp for to makyn and swymen on the se,
   Vpon the water both wood and coolde.
   And viij sowles ther savyd shulde be
   And i peyre of everich bestys in brynge.
   Whan xl^{ti} days the flode had flowe
75 Than sente Noe out a crowe,
   And after hym he sent a dowe
   That brouth ryth good tydyng.

3RD HERALD   Of Abraham is the fyfte pagent
   And of Ysaac his sone so fre—
80 How that he shulde with fere be brent
   And slayn with swerd, as ye shal se.
   Abraham toke, with good atent,
   His sone Ysaac and knelyd on kne;
   His suerd was than ful redy bent,
85 And thouth his chylde ther offered shuld be
   Upon an hyll full ryff.

Than God toke tent to his good wyl
And sent an angel ryth sone hym tyl
And bad Abraham a shep to kyl—
90   And savyd his chyldys lyff.

1ST HERALD   The sexte pagent is of Moyses
And of tweyn tabelys that God hym took
In the which were wrete, with-out les,
The lawes of God to lerne and lok;
95   And how God charged hym be wordys, these
The lawes to lerne al of that book,
Moyses than doth nevyr more sese
But prechyth duly, bothe yere and woke,
The lawes as I yow telle—
100   The ten comaundementys alle be-dene;
In oure play ye shal hem sene,
To alle tho that there wyl bene,
If that ye thenke to duelle.

2ND HERALD   Of the gentyl Jesse rote
105   The sefnt pagent, for sothe, shal ben;
Out of the which doth sprynge oure bote,
As in prophecye we redyn and sen;
Kyngys and prophetys, with wordys ful sote,
Schull prophesye al of a qwen,
110   The which shal staunch oure stryff and moote,
And wynnen us welthe, with-outyn wen,
In hevyn to abyde.
They shal prophecye of a mayde—
All fendys of here shal be affrayde—
115   Here sone shal save us, be not dismayde,
With hese woundys wyde.

3RD HERALD   Of the grete bushop Abyacar
The tende pagent shal be, with-out lesyng;
The which comaundyth men to be war
120   And brynge here douterys to dew weddyng;

---

92. And of the two tablets which God gave to him.

111-12 And gain for us happiness, beyond our expectations (or deserts), by allowing us to live in heaven.

All that ben xiiij yere and more,
To maryage he byddyth hem bryng.
Wher-evyr thei be, he chargyth sore
That thei not fayle, for no lettyng:
125   The lawe byddyth so than.
Than Joachym and Anne so mylde
Thei brynge forthe Mary, that blyssyd chylde;
But she wold not be de-fylyde
With spot nor wem of man.
130   In chastyte that blysful mayde
Avowyd there here lyff to lede;
Than is the busshop sore dysmayde
And wonderyth sore al of this dede.
He knelyd to God, as it is sayde,
135   And prayth than for help and rede.
Than seyth an angel: 'Be not a-frayde.
Of this dowte take thou no drede,
But for the kynrede of Davyd thou sende;
Lete hem come with here offryng
140   And in here handys white yerdys brynge.
Loke whose yerde doth floure and sprynge,
And he shal wedde that mayden hende.'

IST HERALD   In the x^{te} pagent, sothe to say,
A masangere forthe is sent.
145   Davyd is kynrede, without delay,
They come ful sone with good entent.
Whan Joseph offeryd his yerde that day,
Anon ryth forth, in present,
The ded styk do floure ful gay.
150   And than Joseph to wedlok went,
Ryth as the angel bad.
Than he plyth to his wyff
In chastyte to ledyn here lyff.
The busshop toke here iij maydonys ryff—
155   Som comforte there she hadde.

---

145. Those of the kindred of David.
154. The bishop gave her three female attendants.

2ND HERALD In the xi ^{de} pagent goth Gabryell
      And doth salute Our Lady fre.
      Than grett with chylde, as I yow tell,
      That blyssyd mayde, for sothe, is she.
  160 Tho iij maydenys, that with here dwelle,
      Here gret spech but noon thei se.
      Than they suppose that sum angell,
      Goddys masangere, that it shuld be.
      And thus
  165 The Holy Gost in here is lyth
      And Goddys sone in here is pygth.
      The aungell doth telle what he shal hyght,
      And namyth the chylde Jhesus.

THE PROCLAMATION continues for another 360 lines until 41 pageants have been announced for 'Sunday next' at '6 of the bell' when the 'play begins in N. town'.

---

161. (They) hear a loud voice but see no-one.

II. *The Murder of Abel*

Mactatio Abel is the second pageant in the *Towneley Cycle of Plays* and, according to a sixteenth-century hand in the right-hand margin opposite the title of the play, it was presented by the Company of Glovers. This play is the first of the so-called Wakefield Group of six pageants included within the Towneley Cycle; the other five are supposed to have been composed by the dramatist known as the 'Wakefield Master', but only parts of *Mactatio Abel* are attributed to his hand. The original dialect of the play—probably composed 1420–50—was that of the North-east Midlands. Stage directions are editorial. (See *The Wakefield Pageants*, ed. A. C. Cawley, Manchester U.P., 1958.)
MS: *Huntington Library, HM 1.*

Servant (Pike-harnes) Cain Abel God

SERVANT

    All hayll, all hayll, both blithe and glad,
    For here com I, a mery lad;
    Be peasse youre dyn, my master bad,
    Or els the dwill you spede.
5   Wote ye not I com before?
    Bot who that janglis any more
    He must blaw my blak hoill bore,
    Both behynd and before,
    Till his tethe blede.
10   Felows, here I you forbede
    To make nother nose ne cry;
    Who so is so hardy to do that dede
    The dwill hang hym up to dry.

    Gedlyngis, I am a fulle grete wat;
15   A good yoman my master hat,
    Full well ye all hym ken;
    Begyn he with you for to stryfe,
    Certis, then mon ye never thryfe;
    Bot I trow, bi God on life,
20   Som of you ar his men.

3–4. Silence your noise, my master commands, or else go to devil!
7. He will have to play the trumpet on my dirty hole.
17–18. If he were to fight with you, take my word for it, you would get the worse of it.

Bot let youre lippis cover youre ten,
Harlottis, everichon,
For if my master com, welcom hym then.
Farewell, for I am gone.   *Exit Servant.*

Enter Cain.

CAYN   25   Io furth, Greyn-horne! and war oute, Gryme!
Drawes on! God gif you ill to tyme.
Ye stand as ye were fallen in swyme;
What! Will ye no forther, mare?
War, let me se how Down will draw;
          30   Yit, shrew, yit, pull on a thraw.
What! it semys for me ye stand none aw.
I say, Donnyng, go fare.
A, ha! God gif the soro and care.
Lo! now hard she what I saide.
          35   Now yit art thou the warst mare
In plogh that ever I haide.
How! Pike-harnes, how! com heder, belife!
                              Enter Servant.

SERVANT   I fend, Godis forbot, that ever thou thrife.
CAYN   What, boy, shal I both hold and drife?
          40   Heris thou not how I cry?
SERVANT   Say, Mall and Stott, will ye not go?
Lemyng, Morell, White-horne; Io!
Now will ye not se how thay hy?
CAYN   Gog gif the sorow, boy; want of mete it gars.
SERVANT   45   Thare provand, sir, for thi, I lay behynd thare ars,
And tyes them fast bi the nekis,
With many stanys in thare hekis.
CAYN   That shall bi thi fals chekis.   *Hits him.*
SERVANT   And have agane as right.   *Returns the blow.*
CAYN   50   I am thi master; wilt thou fight?

---

25. Greyhorn, Gryme, Donning, Mall, Stott, Lemyng, Morell, Whitehorn,
are the names of horses in the plough team.

31. It looks as though you are not afraid of me.

48. Your false face shall pay for that.

SERVANT		Yai, with the same mesure and weght
		That I boro will I qwite.
CAYN		We! now nothyng, bot call on tyte,
		That we had ployde this land.
SERVANT	55	Harrer, Morell, io furth, hyte.
		And let the plogh stand. *He gives up (and leaves).*

Enter Abell.

ABELL		God, as he both may and can,
		Spede the, brother, and thi man.
CAYN		Com kis myne ars! Me list not ban;
	60	As welcom standis theroute.
		Thou shuld have bide til thou were cald;
		Com nar, and other drife or hald –
		And kys the dwillis toute.
		Go grese thi shepe under the toute,
	65	For that is the moste lefe.
ABELL		Broder, ther is none hereaboute
		That wold the any grefe.
		Bot, leif brother, here my sawe:
		It is the custom of oure law,
	70	All that wyrk as the wise
		Shall worship God with sacrifice.
		Oure fader us bad, oure fader us kend,
		That oure tend shuld be brend.
		Com furth brothere, and let us gang
	75	To worship God. We dwell full lang.
		Gif we hym parte of oure fee,
		Corne or catall, wheder it be.
		And therfor, brother, let us weynd,
		And first clens us from the feynd
	80	Or we make sacrifice—
		Then blis withoutten end
		Get we for oure servyce,
		Of hym that is oure saulis leche.

53-4. Oh! No more now; keep shouting (at the horses) until we have ploughed this land.

59-60. I don't want to curse, but you are quite welcome to stay away.

65. That's the best job for you.

70. All who live by (the teaching) of the wise.

B

CAYN

    How! let furth youre geyse, the fox will preche.
85 How long wilt thou me appech
    With thi sermonyng?
    Hold thi tong, yit I say,
    Even ther the good wife strokid the hay;
    Or sit downe in the dwill way
90 With thi vayn carpyng.
    Shuld I leife my plogh and all thyng
    And go with the to make offeryng?
    Nay! thou fyndys me not so mad.
    Go to the dwill, and say I bad.
95 What gifys God the to rose hym so?
    Me gifys he noght bot soro and wo.

ABELL

    Caym, leife this vayn carpyng,
    For God giffys the all thi lifyng.

CAYN

    Yit boroed I never a farthyng
100 Of hym, here my hend.

ABELL

    Brother, as elders have us kend,
    First shuld we tend with oure hend,
    And to his lofyng sithen be brend.

CAYN

    My farthyng is in the preest hand
105 Syn last tyme I offyrd.

ABELL

    Leif brother, let us be walkand;
    I wold oure tend were profyrd.

CAYN

    We! wherof shuld I tend, leif brothere?
    For I am ich yere wars then othere –

---

84. Reminiscent of a proverbial saying. Cain's adaptation is ironical: 'Ha, ha. Release your geese (to form a congregation for) the fox who is about to preach to them.'

88. An obvious, if obscure piece of vulgarity, as the next line suggests (?Take a running jump!)

94–5. And say I (sent) you. What has God given you that you should praise him for it?

100. Take my hand (as a pledge of my truth).

103. And then our offering should be burned to His glory. (This plain statement indicates to the audience—and the actors—the action later in the play.)

109. Each year's (yield) is worse than that of the previous year. Cain is presented to the audience as a typical English farmer who makes the usual exasperated grumbles about bad weather, poor crops, poverty and, in particular, the exorbitant demands of the Church for tithes. The payment of tithes was a

	110

110 Here my trouth, it is none othere.
    My wynnyngis ar bot meyn,
    No wonder if that I be leyn;
    Full long till hym I may me meyn
    For, bi hym that me dere boght,
115 I traw that he will leyn me noght.

ABELL   Yis, all the good thou has in wone
    Of Godis grace is bot a lone.

CAYN   Lenys he me, as come thrift apon the so?
    For he has ever yit beyn my fo;
120 For had he my freynd beyn,
    Other gatis it had beyn seyn.
    When all mens corn was fayre in feld
    Then was myne not worth a neld;
    When I shuld saw, and wantyd seyde,
125 And of corn had full grete neyde,
    Than gaf he me none of his;
    No more will I gif hym of this.
    Hardely hold me to blame
    Bot if I serve hym of the same.

ABELL 130 Leif brother, say not so,
    Bot let us further togeder go;
    Good brother, let us weynd sone;
    No longer here I rede we hone.

CAYN   Yei, yei, thou jangyls waste;
135 The dwill me spede if I have hast,
    As long as I may lif,
    To dele my good or gif
    Ather to God or yit to man
    Of any good that ever I wan.

---

constant source of friction throughout the middle ages and continued after the Dissolution of the Monasteries. (See G. G. Coulton, *Medieval Village, Manor, and Monastery*, Chapter XX, The Academy Library, Harper; New York, 1960.)
    118. He lends to me? Can you say that honestly (as you hope to thrive)?
    124. And was short of seed (for sowing).
    128–9. You can certainly take me to task if I don't pay him back in the same (coin).
    134. You are wasting your breath.

	140	For had I giffen away my goode,
		Then myght I go with a ryffen hood;
		And it is better hold that I have
		Then go from doore and crave.
ABELL		Brother, com furth in Godis name,
	145	I am full ferd that we get blame;
		Hy we fast that we were thore.
CAYN		We! ryn on, in the dwills nayme, before!
		Wemay, man, I hold the mad.
		Wenys thou now that I list gad
	150	To gif away my warldis aght?
		The dwill hym spede that me so taght!
		What nede had I my travell to lose,
		To were my shoyn and ryfe my hose?
ABELL		Dere brother, hit were grete wonder
	155	That I and thou shuld go in sonder;
		Then wold oure fader have grete ferly—
		Ar we not brether, thou and I?
CAYN		No, bot cry on, cry, whyls the thynk good;
		Here my trowth, I hold the woode.
	160	Wheder that he be blithe or wroth,
		To dele my good is me full lothe.
		I have gone oft on softer wise
		Ther I trowed som prow wold rise.
		Bot well I se, go must I nede—
	165	Now weynd before, ill myght thou spede,
		Syn that we shall algatis go.
ABELL		Leif brother, whi sais thou so?
		Bot go we furth both togeder;
		Blissid be God we have fare weder.

They go across to the altar of sacrifice.

CAYN	170	Lay downe thi trussell apon this hill.

---

146. Let us hurry so that we get there (in time).

149–50. Do you expect me to rush about in order to give away my worldly possessions?

158. Keep shouting as long as it suits you.

162–3. I have often gone (before to sacrifice) without protest because I had thought to gain some (personal) advantage from it.

ABELL   Forsoth broder, so I will:
                 God of heven, take it to good.
CAYN   Thou shall tend first, if thou were wood.
ABELL (*kneeling*)   God that shope both erth and heven,
175   I pray to the thou here my steven,
                 And take in thank, if thi will be,
                 The tend that I offre here to the;
                 For I gif it in good entent
                 To the, my Lord, that all has sent.
180   I bren it now, with stedfast thoght,
                                           Setting it alight.
                 In worship of hym that all has wroght.
CAYN   Ryse! let me now, syn thou has done;
                 Lord of heven, thou here my boyne   *Kneeling.*
                 And over, Goddis forbot, be to the
185   Thank or thew to kun me;
                 For, as browke I thise two shankys,
                 It is full sore, myne unthankys,
                 The teynd that I here gif to the,
                 Of corn or thyng—that newys me.
190   Bot now begyn will I then—
                 Syn I must nede my tend to bren.
                 Oone shefe, oone, and this makys two,
                 Bot nawder of thise may I forgo:
Counts out his sheaves, selecting the worst for God and keeping the best
                                           for himself.
                 Two, two, now this is thre,
195   Yei, this also shall leif with me:
                 For I will chose and best have.
                 This hold I thrift of all this thrafe.
                 Wemo, wemo, foure, lo, here!
                 Better groued me none this yere.
200   At yere tyme I sew fayre corn,
                 Yit was it sich when it was shorne—
                                   Showing it to the audience.

184–5. And God forbid that you should ever show me thanks or courtesy.
186. As I enjoy the use of my two legs.
197. I consider all of these (twenty-four) sheaves to be (my share of) my earnings.

Thystyls and brerys, yei grete plente,
And all kyn wedis that myght be.
Four shefis, foure, lo, this makis fyfe—
205   Deyll I fast thus long or I thrife.
Fyfe and sex, now this is sevyn—
Bot this gettis never God of heven;
Nor none of thise foure, at my myght,
Shall never com in Godis sight.
210   Sevyn, sevyn, now this is aght.

ABELL   Cam, brother, thou art not God betaght.

CAYN   We! therfor is it that I say;
For I will not deyle my good away;
Bot had I gyffen hym this to teynd
215   Then wold thou say he were my freynd;
Bot I thynk not, bi my hode,
To departe so lightly fro my goode.
We! aght, aght, and neyn, and ten is this;
We! this may we best mys.
220   Gif hym that, that ligis thore—
It goyse agans myn hart full sore.

ABELL   Cam! teynd right of all bedeyn.

CAYN   We lo! xij, xv, and xvj—

ABELL   Caym, thou tendis wrang, and of the warst.

CAYN   225   We! com nar, and hide myne een.
In the wenyand, wist ye now at last.
Or els will thou that I wynk?
Than shall I doy no wrong, me thynk.
Here, Cain closes his eyes and then examines the result.
Let me se now how it is—
230   Lo, yit I hold me paide;
I teyndyd wonder well bi ges,
And so even I laide.

---

205. If I part with them as fast as this, I'll never become rich.
208. If I can help it, not one of these four.
220. Shall I give him that (good sheaf) which lies there?
222. Pay the exact tithe of all your goods.
225. Come nearer and cover up my eyes (if you dare?). Cain then proceeds to count the last few blindly and (l. 230) admits, 'I am satisfied with the results'.
232. I've actually divided it quite fairly.

ABELL		Came, of God me thynke thou has no drede.
CAYN		Now, and he get more—the dwill me spede—
	235	As mych as oone reepe;
		For that cam hym full light chepe;
		Not as mekill, grete ne small,
		As he myght wipe his ars with all.
		For that, and this that lyys here,
	240	Have cost me full dere;
		Or it was shorne and broght in stak
		Had I many a wery bak.
		Therfor aske me no more of this,
		For I have giffen that my will is.
ABELL	245	Cam, I rede thou tend right
		For drede of hym that sittis on hight.
CAYN		How that I tend, rek the never a deill,
		Bot tend thi skabbid shepe wele;
		For if thou to my teynd tent take,
	250	It bese the wars for thi sake.
		Thou wold I gaf hym this shefe, or this sheyfe;
		Na, nawder of thise ij wil I leife.
		Bot take this. Now has he two,
		And for my saull now mot it go,
	255	Bot it gos sore agans my will—
		And shal he like full ill.
ABELL		Cam, I reyde thou so teynd
		That God of heven be thi freynd.
CAYN		My freynd?—na, not bot if he will;
	260	I did hym never yit bot skill.
		If he be never so my fo,
		I am avisid gif hym no mo.
		Bot chaunge thi conscience, as I do myn.
		Yit teynd thou not thi mesel swyne?

---

236. All that He has received has been obtained at bargain rates.
241. Before it was reaped and carried into the stackyard.
248. You go and attend properly to your own scabby sheep.
254-5. I suppose I must let it go for the good of my soul—but against my inclination.
262. I have decided to give him no more.
264. Aren't you now going to offer (God) a tenth of your rotten swine?

ABELL	265	If thou teynd right, thou mon it fynde.
CAYN		Yei, kys the dwills ars behynde.
		The dwill hang the bi the nek.
		How that I teynd, never thou rek.
		Will thou not yit hold thi peasse?
	270	Of this janglyng I reyde thou seasse:
		And teynd I well, or tend I ill,
		Bere the even and speke bot skill.
		Bot now syn thou has teyndid thyne,
		Now will I set fyr on myne.
	275	We! out! haro! help to blaw!

Blows on the dying flame.

		It will not bren for me, I traw.
		Puf! this smoke dos me mych shame—
		Now bren, in the dwillys name
		A! what dwill of hell is it?
	280	Almost had myne breth beyn dit.
		Had I blawen oone blast more
		I had beyn choked right thore.
		It stank like the dwill in hell,
		That longer ther myght I not dwell.
ABELL	285	Cam, this is not worth oone leke;
		Thy tend shuld bren withoutten smeke.
CAYN		Com kys the dwill right in the ars.
		For the it brens bot the wars.
		I wold that it were in thi throte,
	290	Fyr, and shefe, and ich a sprote. *God speaks from*
GOD		Cam, whi art thou so rebell [*above.*
		Agans thi brother Abell?
		Thar thou nowther flyte ne chyde—
		If thou tend right, thou gettis thi mede.
	295	And be thou sekir, if thou teynd fals,
		Thou bese alowed ther-after als.

---

265. If you make the correct offering God will show his approval.

271–2. Whether I offer a fitting or a poor tithe, you keep calm and speak when you have something sensible to say.

288. Because of you it burns so poorly.

293. There is no need for you to quarrel or curse.

296. You shall be rewarded later on according to your offering.

CAYN		Whi, who is that Hob-over-the-wall?
		We! who was that that piped so small?
		Com go we hens, for parels all.
	300	God is out of hys wit.
		Com furth Abell, and let us weynd.
		Me thynk that God is not my freynd;
		On land then will I flyt.
ABELL		A, Caym, brother, that is ill done.
CAYN	305	No; bot go we hens sone;
		And if I may, I shall be
		Ther as God shall not me see.
ABELL		Dere brother, I will fayre
		On feld ther oure bestis ar,
	310	To looke if thay be holgh or full.
CAYN		Na, na, abide; we have a craw to pull;
		Hark, speke with me or thou go.
		What, wenys thou to skape so?
		We! na! I aght the a fowll dispyte
	315	And now is tyme that I hit qwite.
ABEL		Brother, whi art thou so to me in ire?
CAYN		We! Theyf. Whi brend thi tend so shyre,
		Ther myne did bot smoked
		Right as it wold us both have choked?
ABEL	320	Godis will I trow it were
		That myn brened so clere.
		If thyne smoked, am I to wite?
CAYN		We! yei! that shal thou sore abite.
		With cheke-bon, or that I blyn,
	325	Shal I the and thi life twyn. *He attacks Abel.*
		So lig down ther and take thi rest—
		Thus shall shrewes be chastysed best.
ABELL		Veniance, veniance, Lord, I cry!
		For I am slayn, and not gilty.

---

297. Hob—a variant of Robin—was a popular and mischievous character in North English folk-tales. Hobgoblin is a variant of Robin Goodfellow (cf. Shakespeare's Puck). Cain hears a voice but cannot see the speaker.

299. Let's move away from here and avoid all dangers.

311. Stay here. We have a bone to pick.

314. I am indebted to you for a severe injury (i.e. God's rebuke).

317. Why did your offering burn so brightly?

B*

CAYN   330   Yei, ly ther old shrew; ly ther, ly!
                   And if any of you thynk I did amyss,

To the audience.

                   I shal it amend wars then it is—
                   That all men may it se:
                   Well wars then it is,
    335   Right so shall it be.
                   Bot now, syn he is broght on slepe,
                   Into som hole fayn wold I crepe;
                   For ferd I qwake and can no rede—
                   For be I taken, I be bot dede.
    340   Here will I lig this fourty dayes,
                   And I shrew hym that me fyrst rayse.

GOD (*from above*)   Caym, Caym!
CAYN   Who is that that callis me?
                   I am yonder, may thou not se?

GOD   345   Caym, where is thi brother Abell?
CAYN   What askis thou me? I trow at hell—
                   At hell I trow he be;
                   Who so were ther then myght he se—
                   Or somwhere fallen on slepyng.
    350   When was he in my kepyng?
GOD   Caym, Caym, thou was wode;
                   The voyce of thi brotheris blode
                   That thou has slayn on fals wise,
                   From erth to heven venyance cryse.
    355   And, for thou has broght thi brother downe,
                   Here I gif the my malison.
CAYN   Yei, dele aboute the, for I will none,
                   Or take it the when I am gone.
                   Syn I have done so mekill syn,

---

332. I shall (have to) make amends for this crime in a manner that will be worse than the crime itself.

338. I tremble for fear and don't know what to do.

345. God's speech follows the Biblical narrative closely. (See *Genesis* 5: 9–12.)

346–8. In hell, I expect. [Then Cain says in an aside to the audience] 'I really believe him to be in hell; if you went there you'd see him.'

357. Go on. Scatter it (i.e. God's curse) on all sides—I don't want any of it. And take it back again for yourself once I've left.

360 That I may not thi mercy wyn,
And thou thus dos me from thi grace,
I shall hyde me fro thi face;
And where so any man may fynd me,
Let hym slo me hardely;

365 And where so any man may me meyte,
Ayther bi sty or yit bi strete;
And hardely, when I am dede,
Bery me in Gudeboure at the quarell hede;
For, may I pas this place in quarte,

370 Bi all men set I not a fart.

GOD   Nay, Caym, it bese not so—
I will that no man other slo;
For he that sloys yong or old
It shall be punyshid sevenfold.

CAYN 375 No force, I wote wheder I shall:
In hell, I wote, mon be my stall.
It is no boyte mercy to crave;
For if I do, I mon none have.
Bot this cors I wold were hid;

380 For som man myght com at ungayn—
'Fle fals shrew,' wold he bid,
And weyn I had my brother slayn.
Bot were Pike-harnes, my knafe, here,
We shuld bery hym both in fere.
                              Calls to his boy.

385 How Pyke-harnes! Scape-thryft! how, Pike-
harnes, how!
        Servant re-enters, shouting, 'Master, Master!'
CAYN   Harstow, boy? Ther is a podyng in the pot.
Take the that, boy; tak the that.   *Strikes him.*

---

368. There are a few references to Goody-bower and its quarry in Wakefield documents.

372. It is not my will that one man should kill another.

376. My ultimate destination, I know, must be in hell.

380-2. It seems part of the author's purpose to suggest that, to some extent, Cain is quite incapable of realizing his own part in Abel's death: on the other hand, these three lines could be a leering aside to the audience, in true Victorian melodramatic style.

386. There's immediate work to do.

SERVANT		I shrew thi ball under thi hode,
		If thou were my syre of flesh and blode;
	390	All the day to ryn and trott
		And ever amang thou strykeand—
		Thus am I comen bofettis to fott.
CAYN		Peas, man, I did it bot to use my hand.
		Bot harke, boy, I have a counsell to the to say;
	395	I slogh my brother this same day.
		I pray the, good boy, and thou may,
		To ryn away with the bayn.
SERVANT		We! out apon the, thefe!
		Has thou thi brother slayn?
CAYN	400	Peasee, man, for Godis payn!
		I saide it for a skaunce.
SERVANT		Yey, bot for ferde of grevance
		Here I the forsake;
		We mon have a mekill myschaunce
	405	And the bayles us take.
CAYN		A, sir, I cry you mercy! Scasse!
		And I shall make you a releasse.
SERVANT		What, wilt thou cry my peasse
		Throughout this land?
CAYN	410	Yey, that I gif God a vow, belife.
SERVANT		How will thou do long or thou thrife?
CAYN		Stand up, my good boy, belife,
		And thaym peasse, both man and wife;
		And who so will do after me
	415	Full slape of thrift then shal he be.
		Bot thou must be my good boy,
		And cry 'oyes, oyes, oy!'

Throughout this exchange, Cain utters the correct formula and the servant
mocks him to the audience.

SERVANT	Browes, browes, to thi boy.

388–9. I'd curse the head under your cap, even if you were my own father.
392. This way all I get is blows.
404–5. We shall have bad luck, indeed, if the sheriff's men catch us.
408–9. Will you have my special protection proclaimed throughout the land?
411. How long will it be before you carry it out successfully?

CAYN		I commaund you in the kyngis nayme,
SERVANT	420	And in my masteres, fals Cayme—
CAYN		That no man at thame fynd fawt ne blame.
SERVANT		Yey, cold rost is at my masteres hame.
CAYN		Nowther with hym nor with his knafe,
SERVANT		What! I hope my master rafe—
CAYN	425	For thay ar trew, full many fold;
SERVANT		My master suppys no coyle bot cold.
CAYN		The kyng wrytis you untill.
SERVANT		Yit ete I never half my fill.
CAYN		The kyng will that thay be safe,
SERVANT	430	Yey, a draght of drynke fayne wold I hayfe.
CAYN		At thare awne will let tham wafe;
SERVANT		My stomak is redy to receyfe.
CAYN		Loke no man say to theym, on nor other;
SERVANT		This same is he that slo his brother.
CAYN	435	Byd every man thaym luf and lowt,
SERVANT		Yey, ill spon weft ay comes foule out.
CAYN (*to the boy*)		Long or thou get thi hoyse and thou go thus aboute.

(Continues with his proclamation)

		Byd every man theym pleasse to pay.
SERVANT		Yey, gif Don, thyne hors, a wisp of hay.

The boy climbs up out of Cain's reach.

CAYN	440	We! com downe in twenty dwill way;
		The dwill I the betake.
		For bot it were Abell, my brothere,
		Yit knew I never thi make.
SERVANT		Now old and yong, or that ye weynd,

To the audience from his perch.

419–438. Cain imitates here a royal proclamation of pardon (*peasse*, line 413), which would release him from the consequences of his murder. His servant's derogatory imitation of Cain's legal formulae is a source of clowning and a direct comment on Cain's moral blindness.

427. It is the king that writes to you.

429, 431. The king wishes that they be given safe-conduct (be allowed to wander where they please and commands . . .).

433. That no man say anything (i.e. accusation of guilt) to either of them.

437. It will be a long time before you prosper (i.e. get your hose), if you carry on like this.

445   The same blissyng withoutten end,
      All sam then shall ye have,
      That God of heven my master has giffen;
      Browke it well, whils that ye liffen,
      He vowche it full well safe.

CAYN   450   Com downe, yit, in the dwillis way,
      And angre me no more   *The boy comes down.*
      And take yond plogh, I say,
      And weynd the furth fast before
      And I shall, if I may,

455   Tech the another lore:
      I warn the lad, for ay,
      Fro now furth, evermore,
      That thou greve me noght.
      For, bi Godis sydis, if thou do,

460   I shall hang the apon this plo,
      With this rope; lo, lad, lo!   *Threatens him.*
      By hym that me dere boght.
             The boy goes off with the plough.

To the audience   Now fayre well, felows all,
      For I must nedis weynd

465   And to the dwill be thrall
      Warld withoutten end.
      Ordand ther is my stall
      With Sathanas the feynd;
      Ever ill myght hym befall

470   That theder me commend
      This tyde.
      Fare well les and fare well more,
      For now and ever more.
      I will go me to hyde.   *Exit Cain.*

After the last line the manuscript contains this comment in Latin: 'Here ends the Killing of Abel. Noah follows.'

---

449. May He truly grant it to you.

462. Cain, an Old Testament character and the archetypal murderer, swears by Christ who redeemed mankind: this is an apt illustration of the vivid contemporaneity of all the Miracle Plays.

III. Noah

The following text is number '4' in the *Ludus Coventriae* and comes immediately after the pageant of *Cain and Abel*. All names of characters and all stage directions in the manuscript are given in Latin. The dialect is Northern of the late fifteenth century.

MS: British Museum, Cotton Vespasian D. VIII.

Enter NOE

God of his goodnesse and of grace grounde,
By whoys gloryous power all thyng is wrought,
In whom all vertu plenteuously is founde,
With-owtyn whos wyl may be ryth nought,
5 Thy servauntys save, Lord, from synful sownde,
In wyl, in werk, in dede, and in thouht.
Oure welth in woo lete nevyr be fownde.
Us help, Lord, from synne that we be in brought,
Lord God ful of myght.
10 Noe, serys, my name is knowe,
My wyf and my chyldere here on rowe;
To God we pray, with hert ful lowe,
To plese hym in his syght.
In me, Noe, the secunde age
15 In dede be-gynnyth, as I yow say:
After Adam with-outyn langage
The secunde fadyr am I, in fay.
But men of levyng be so owt-rage
Bothe be nyght and eke be day
20 That, lesse than synne the soner swage,
God wyl be vengyd on us sum way.
In dede
Ther may no man go ther-owte
But synne regnyth in every rowte:

---

1. God, the foundation of virtue and of grace.
4. Without whose will nothing at all can exist.
8. Help us, Lord, so that we are rescued from sin.
11. As the other actors enter the stage in sequence (*on rowe*) from an 'inner stage', Noah points to them. The actors then come forward and introduce themselves upstage.
20. That, unless sin is quickly abandoned.

25 In every place rownde a-bowte
     Cursydnes doth sprynge and sprede.

NOE'S WIFE   All-myghty God, of his gret grace,
     Enspyre men with hertely wyll
     For to sese of here trespace.

30 For synfull levyng oure sowle shal spyll.
     Synne offendyth God in his face
     And a-grevyth oure Lorde full ylle;
     It causyth to man ryght grett manace
     And scrapyth hym out of lyvys bylle—

35 That blyssyd book.
     What man in synne doth all wey scleppe,
     He shall gon to helle ful deppe;
     Than shal he nevyr after creppe
     Out of that brennyng brook.

40 I am your wyff, your childeryn these be;
     On to us tweyn it doth longe
     Hem to teche in all degre
     Synne to for-sakyn and werkys wronge.
     Therfore, fere, for love of me,

45 Enforme hem wele, evyr amonge,
     Synne to for-sake and vanyte,
     And vertu to folwe, that thei ffonge
     Oure Lord God to plese.

NOE   I warne yow childeryn, on and all,
50 Drede oure Lord God in hevy hall
     And in no forfete that we ne fall
     Oure Lord for to dysplese.

SHEM   A, dere fadyr, God for-bede
     That we shulde do, in ony wyse,

---

34. And erases his name from the Book of Life.

41–3. It is the task of both of us to instruct them in every possible way to give up sin and wrong-doing.

53. Shem, like his mother, and the rest of the speakers in this pageant are never realized as naturalistic characters: the different voices are employed to present the well-known story and to draw the appropriate lessons from it. The dramatist is applying the techniques familiar to his audience from mural decorations within the churches and on tapestries.

55 Ony werke of synful dede
   Oure Lord God that shulde a-gryse.
   My name is Shem, your son of prise.
   I shal werke aftere your rede;
   And also, wyff, the weyll awyse
60 Wykkyd werkys that thou non brede,
   Never in no degre.

SHEM'S WIFE   For-sothe, sere, by Goddys grace,
               I shal me kepe from all trespace
               That shulde offende Goddys face
65   Be help of the Trynyte.

CHAM   I am Cham, your secunde son,
               And purpose me, be Goddys myght,
               Nevyr suche a dede for to don
               That shuld a-greve God in syght.

CHAM'S WIFE 70 I pray to God, me grawnt this bone,
               That he me kepe in such a plyght,
               Mornynge, hevenynge, mydday and none,
               I to affendyn hym day nor nyght.
               Lord God I the pray,
75   Bothe wakynge and eke in slepe,
               Gracyous God, thou me keppe
               That I nevyr in daunger crepe
               On dredfull domys day.

JAPHET   Japhet thi iij^de sone is my name.
80   I pray to God wher-so we be
               That he us borwe fro synfull shame
               And in vertuous levynge evyr more kepe me.

JAPHET'S WIFE I am your wyf, and pray the same,
               That God us save on sonde and se;
85   With no grevauns that we hym grame;
               He grawnt us grace synne to fle.
               Lord God now here oure bone.

55-6. Commit any sinful act that would offend our Lord.

59-61. And also, my wife, be very careful that you do not in any way create occasions for sinful acts.

70. I pray to God that he grant me this prayer.

NOE

> Gracyous God, that best may,
> With herty wyl to the we pray
> 90 Thou save us sekyr, bothe nyght and day,
> Synne that we noon done.

GOD (*above*)

> Ow, what menyth this mys-levyng man
> Whiche myn hand made and byldyd in blyssc.
> Synne so sore grevyth me; ya, in certayn,
> 95 I wol be vengyd of this grett mysse.
> Myn aungel dere, thou shalt gan
> To Noe, that my servaunt is.
> A shypp to make on hond to tan
> Thou byd hym swyth for hym and his,
> 100 From drynchyng to save.
> For, as I am God of myght,
> I shal dystroye this werd down-ryght.
> Here synne so sore grevyth me in syght
> Thei shal no mercy have.

> 105 *Fecisse hominem nunc penitet me—*
> That I made man sore doth me rewe;
> Man handwerk to sle, sore grevyth me,
> But that here synne here deth doth brewe.
> Go, sey to Noe as I bydde the:
> 110 Hym-self, his wyf, his chylderyn trewe—
> Tho viij sowlys in shyp to be.
> Thei shul not drede the flodys flowe—
> The flod shal harme them nowht.
> Of all fowlys and bestys thei take a peyre,
> 115 In shypp to save, both foule and fayere,
> From all dowtys and gret dyspeyre
> This vengeauns or it be wrought.

---

88. Gracious God, who dost all things for the best.

96–97. In the Bible narrative (*Genesis* 6–9) God speaks directly to Noah.

98–99. You command him to set about building a ship quickly for himself and his (family).

108. Except that their (own) sin brings about their death.

115–117. At this point in the text the handwriting is squeezed together: the syntax, too, is a little unclear. Probably—'They shall take a pair of all beasts and birds, clean and unclean, and save them in a ship before this vengeance is accomplished and (thus save them) from all doubts and despair.'

ANGEL *(to Noe)*   Noe! Noe! A shypp loke thou make—
                    And many a chaumbyr thou shalt have therinne;
120   Of every kyndys best, a cowpyl thou take
                    With-in the shypp bord—here lyvys to wynne.
                    For God is sore grevyd with man for his synne
                    That all this wyde werd shal be dreynt with flood,
                    Saff thou and thi wyff shal be kept from this gynne
125   And also thi chylderyn, with here vertuys good.

NOE   How shuld I have wytt, a shypp for to make?
                    I am of ryght grett age, V.C. yere olde.
                    It is not for me this werk to undyrtake;
                    For feynnesse of age my leggys gyn folde.

ANGEL   130   This dede for to do, be bothe blythe and bolde;
                    God shal enforme the and rewle the ful ryght.
                    Of byrd and of beste take, as I the tolde,
                    A peyr in to the shypp, and God shal the qwyght.

NOE   I am ful redy as God doth me bydde,
135   A shypp for to make, be myght of his grace.
                    Alas, that for synne it shal be so be-tydde
                    That vengeauns of flood shal werke this manase:
                    God is sore grevyd with oure grett tresspas
                                                    To his family
                    That with wylde watyr the werd shal be dreynt.
140   A shyppe for to make, now lete us hens pas,
                    That God agens us of synne have no compleynt.

*Noah and his family leave the stage in order to fetch their ship (which would
not be in the playing area).*
Then Lameth enters, being led by a boy, and speaks.

124-5. Except that you and your wife and your virtuous children shall be
saved from this plan (of destruction).
129. Because of the feebleness [faintness?—MS reading unclear] of age, my
legs are bent.
131. God shall instruct you and guide you in every way.
136-7. Alas, because of sin it shall come to pass that God shall bring about
this punishment through the vengeance of a flood:
140. Let us now go away from this spot in order to make a ship.

LAMETH   Gret mornyng I make and gret cause I have:
                     Alas, now I se not; for age I am blynde.
                     Blyndenes doth make me of wytt for to rave,
145   Whantynge of eyesyght, in peyn doth me bynde.
                     Whyl I had syht ther myht nevyr man fynde
                     My pere of archerye, in all this werd a-boute.
                     For yitt schet I nevyr at hert, are, nere hynde,
                     But yf that he deyd—of this no man have doute.

150   Lameth the good archere my name was ovyrall;
                     For the best archere myn name dede ever sprede.
                     Record of my boy here wytnes this he shal
                     What merk that were set me, to deth it shuld blede.

BOY   It is trewer, that ye see, maystyn, in dede;
155   For that tyme ye had youre bowe bent in honde
                     If that your prycke had be half a myle in brede,
                     Ye wolde the pryk han hitte, if ye ny had stonde.

LAMETH   I shuld nevyr affaylid, what marke that ever were sett,
                     Whyl that I myght loke and had my clere syght.
160   And yit, as me thynkyth, no man shuld shete bett
                     Than I shuld do now, if myn hand were sett a-ryght.
                     Aspye som marke, boy; my bowe shal I bende wyght
                     And sett myn hand evyn to shete at som best;
                     And I dar ley a wagour his deth for to dyght—
                                                 Bends his bow.
165   The marke shal I hitt: my lyf do I hest.

---

142. Lameth (the O.T. *Lamech*) was a son of Methuselah and father of Noah. (See *Genesis* 4: 18-24, 5: 25-31.) The incident in the play—which allows time for Noah to bring on his ark—is based on a misunderstanding of two verses in the Song of Lamech: 'For I have slain a man to my wounding, and a young man to my hurt. If Cain shall be avenged sevenfold, truly, Lamech seventy and sevenfold.' (*Genesis* 4: 23-4). His blindness is probably deduced from his age (777).

148-9. Believe me, I have never failed to kill any beast—hart, hare, or hind—that I have shot at.

152. My boy here can testify to the fact.

157. You would have hit the target as well as if you had been close to it.

BOY

Undyr yon grett busche, mayster, a best do I se.
Take me thin hand swyth and holde it ful stylle;

The boy guides his arm.

Now is thin hand evyn as evyr it may be—
Drawe up thin takyll, yon best for to kylle.

LAMETH   170   My bowe shal I drawe ryght, with herty wylle;
This brod arwe I shete that best for to sayll.
Now have at that busch, yon best for to spylle.

He shoots and hits Cain, who is at the edge of the stage.

A sharppe schote I shote; ther-of I shal not fayll.

CAYN

Out, out, and alas! myn hert is on sondyr.
175   With a brod arwe I am ded and sclayn.
I dye here on grounde; myn hert is all to tundyr—
With this brod arwe it is clovyn on twayn.

LAMETH

Herke, boy. Cum telle me the trewth in certeyn:
What man is he, that this cry doth thus make.

BOY   180   Caym thou hast kyllyd; I telle the ful pleyn.
With thi sharp shetyng, his deth hath he take.

LAMETH

Have I slayn Cayme? Alas, what have I done?
Thou stynkynge lurdeyn, what hast thou wrought?
Thou art the why I scle hym so sone;
185   Ther-fore shal I kyll the here. Thou skapyst nowght.

Lameth beats the boy to death with his bow.

BOY *(as he dies)*

Out, out! I deye here. My deth is now sought;
This theffe, with his bowe, hath broke my brayn.
Ther may non helpe be; my dethe is me brought.
Ded, here I synke down, as man that is sclayn.

LAMETH   190   Alas! what shal I do, wrecch, wykkyd on woolde;
God wyl be vengyd ful sadly on me.
For deth of Caym, I shal have vii folde
More peyn than he had, that Abell dede sle.

---

171. I shall shoot this broad arrow in order to kill that animal.

184. You are the reason why I have killed him even now (or, possibly, before his time).

190. Miserable, wicked man in this world (that I am).

These to mennys deth full sore bought shal be—
195   Upon all my blood God wyll venge this dede
Where-fore, sore wepyng, hens wyl I fle,
And loke where I may best my hede sone heyde.

Exit Lameth.

Enter Noe with his ship, singing.

NOE   With doolfull hert, syenge, sad and sore,
Grett mornyng I make for this dredful flood;
200   Of man and of best is dreynte, many a skore.
All this werd to spyll, these flodys be ful wood;
And all is for synne of mannys wylde mood
That God hath ordeyned this dredfull vengeaunce.
In this flood spylt is many a mannys blood;
205   For synfull levynge of man we have gret grevauns.
All this hundryd yere, ryght here have I wrought
This schypp for to make, as God dede byd me:
Of all maner bestys, a copyll is in brought
With-in my shypp borde, on-lyve for to be.
210   Ryght longe God hath soferyd, amendyng to se:
All this hundyrd yere, God hath shewyd grace.
Alas, fro gret syn man wyl not fle;
God doth this vengeauns for oure gret trespase.

NOE'S WIFE   Alas, for gret ruthe of this gret vengeaunce;
215   Gret doyl it is to se, this watyr so wyde.
But yit, thankyd be God of this ordenaunce
That we be now savyd, on-lyve to abyde.

SHEM   For grett synne of lechory, all this doth betyde.
Alas, that evyr such synne shulde be wrought.

194–5. The deaths of these two men will be bitterly paid for because God will avenge this deed on all my family.

198. In most of the miracle plays Noah is presented as a man who sings, while he is making the ark and later, at the end of the play, a song of thanksgiving.

201–3. These flood waters are raging madly in order to destroy the world. And it is solely because of man's intemperate (and passionate) behaviour that God has ordained this terrible revenge.

205. This great disaster has come because of man's sinful way of life.

210. God has been tolerant over-long: hoping to see some improvement (in morals).

220   This flood is so gret on every asyde
      That all this wyde werd, to care is now brought.

SHEM'S WIFE   Becawse of chylderyn of God, that weryn good,
      Dede forfete ryght sore, what tyme that thei were
      Synfully compellyd to Caymys blood,
225   Therfore be we now cast in ryght grett care.

CHAM   For synful levynge this werde doth for-fare;
      So grevous vengeauns myght nevyr man se—
      Ovyr all this werd wyde ther is no plot bare;
      With watyr and with flood God vengyd wyll be.

CHAM'S WIFE 230   Rustynes of synne is cawse of these wawys.
      Alas, in this flood this werd shal be lorn;
      For offens to God, brekyng his lawys,
      On rokkys ryght sharp is many a man torn.

JAPHET   So grevous flodys were nevyr yett beforn—
235   Alas, that lechory this vengeauns doth gynne;
      It were well bettyr ever to be unborn
      Than for to forfetyn evyr-more in that synne.

JAPHET'S WIFE   Oure Lord God I thanke of his gret grace,
      That he doth us save from this dredful payn;
240   Hym for to wurchipe, in every stede and place,
      We beth gretly bownde, with myght and with
        mayn.

NOE   xl^{ti} days and nyghtys hath lasted this rayn,
      And xl^{ti} days this grett flood begynnyth to slake;
      This crowe shal I sende out, to seke sum playn.
245   Good tydyngys to brynge, this massage I make.

Noah sends out a crow and, after waiting in vain for its return, he says:

NOE   This crowe on sum careyn is fall, for to ete.
      Therfore a newe masangere I wyll forth now sende:

222–4. Because the children of God, who were (one-time) virtuous, sinned so grievously, because they were compelled to sin because (they had inherited) Cain's blood.

230. The corruption of sin is the reason for these waves.

240–1. It is our bounden duty to honour him everywhere to the best of our ability.

245. I send out this messenger in search of good news.

> Fly forth, thou fayr dove, ovyr these waterys wete
> And aspye aftere sum drye lond, oure mornyng to
>   a-mend.

Here the dove flies away and returns with a sprig of green olive.

NOE   250   Joye now may we make of myrth, that that were
                      frende;
                 A grett olyve bush this dove doth us brynge;
                 For joye of this token, ryght hertyly we tende.
                 Oure Lord God to worchep, a songe lete us synge.

  they all sing these verses:
                 He saw the sea and fled.
            255 On the River Jordan they turned their backs.
                 Not to us, O Lord, not to us,
                 But to Thy name be given the glory.

And so they leave the stage with their ship.

---

49. And look for some dry land (and so) put an end to our sorrow.

250. Because that (act) was favourable (to us).

254-7. The lines here are translated from the Latin of the original.

IV. Balaam and Balak

The pageant of *Balaam and Balak* is the fifth play in *The Chester Plays*, of which there are several copies. The following text, which was copied in 1607, is here presented as an example of the various plays about the Prophets which must have formed an essential link between the Old Testament and the New in every complete cycle of plays. The habit of using every possible incident in the Old Testament to illuminate or support Christian teaching was a vital element in medieval scriptural exegesis. The dialect is a late form of the West Midland M.E. dialect. In the following version, the Latin proper names and stage directions have been translated into English. Occasionally stage directions have been expanded.

MS: British Museum, Harleian 2124.

Enter God and Moses above the level of the stage.

GOD   Moyses, my servaunte life and dere,
               And all the people that be here,
               You wott, in Egipte when you were,
               Out of thralldome I you broughte.
5   I wyll, you honour no God save me,
               Ne mawmentrye none make yee,
               My name in vayne nam not yee—
               For that me lykes naughte.

               I will, you hold your holy daye,
10   And worshipp also, by all waye,
               Father and mother, all that you maye,
               And slaye no man no-where.
               Fornication you shall flee;
               No mens goodes steale yee;
15   Ne in no place abyde ne bee
               Falce wytnes for to beare.

               Your neightboures wyves covettes noughte,
               Servant ne good that he hath boughte
               Oxe ne asse, in deede ne thoughte,
20   Nor any thinge that is his—

---

5. The ten commandments of Moses begin here. Cf. *Exodus* 20: 1-17.

9-10. I command that you keep the Sabbath and, in every way, honour your father and mother.

Ne wrongefullie to have his thinge
Agayne his will and his lykinge.
In all these doe my byddinge,
That you doe not amisse.

The rulers of the synagogue now take up their place on the stage (literally, in loco) and, on behalf of the people, address God and Moses.

RULERS   25   Ah, good Lord, much of mighte,
Thou comes with so great lighte,
We bene so afraide of this sighte,
No man dare speak ne looke.
God is so grym with us to deale,
30   But Moyses, master, with us thou mele—
Els we dyen, many and feele,
So afrayde bene all wee.

Moses now stands on a hill and speaks to the people.

MOYSES   Gods folke, drede you noughte;
To prove you with, God hath this wrought—
35   To make you afrayd, in deede and thoughte
Aye for to avoyde synne.
By this sight you may now see
That he is pereles of postye;
Therfore his teaching look done yee—
40   Thereof that you not blyn.

RULER   Ah, highe Lord, God almighte,
That Moyses shynes wondrous bright!
I may no way, for great lighte,
Now looke upon hym.
45   And horned he semes in our sighte,

23–4. Follow my commandment in these things and you will not sin.

29–30. God is too awe-inspiring for us to have dealings (directly with him) unless you, Moses our teacher, speak for us.

34. God has done this in order to test you.

38–9. That he is unmatched in power and therefore see that you follow his teachings.

45. See *Exodus* 34: 29–35. When Moses descended from Mount Sinai with the laws 'the skin of his face shone'. In the Hebrew text the verb 'shone' is derived from a noun for 'horn' (which is used also in *Psalm* 69: 31). In the Vulgate translation of this passage 'shone' is translated as 'horned'. It is on this

Sith he came to the hyll; dight
Our lawe he hase, I hope aright;
For was he never so grym.

MOYSES   You, Gods folke of Israell,
        50   Harkens to me that loven heale.
              God bade, you sholde doe everye deale
              As that I shall saye:
              Six dayes boldelye worches all,
              The seaventh, Sabaoth you shall call:
        55   That daye, for ought that may befall,
              Hallowed shal be aye.

              That doth not this deede deade shall be;
              In houses, fire shall no man see.
              First fruytes to God offer yee—
        60   For so hym selfe bade.
              Gould and silver offers also—
              Purple, bisse, and other moe—
              To hym that shall save you from woe
              And helpe you in your neede.

EXPOSITOR   65   Lordinges, this comaundment
(to the people)   Was of the Old Testamente,

---

translation that the medieval pictorial representations of Moses with horns were
based. (Compare Michelangelo's sculpture of Moses.) The 'horns' represent the
rays of light from Moses' countenance which caused him to wear a veil when
he spoke to the children of Israel.

51-2. God commanded (that) you should do everything according to my
words.

57. He who does not act in this way shall die.

62. Purple, fine linen, and other (additional fine) things.

65. In several plays in the cycle an Expositor is introduced to interpret,
or comment on the action. In the *Abraham and Isaac* play he enters 'riding',
and presumably he rode up to the stage and delivered his commentary on
horseback. He is obviously conceived as external to the dramatic action and
in some of the MSS of this cycle he is referred to as 'the doctor', which suggests
that the Expositor was dressed as a Doctor of Divinity, suitably qualified to
interpret the scriptures. In other cycles, notably those of Towneley and York,
the dramatists prefer to place such commentaries in the mouths of leading
characters.

And yet is used, with good entente,
With all that good bene.
This storye all, if we shold fong,
70 To playe this moneth, it were to longe;
Wherfore most frutefull there amonge
We taken, as shall be sene.

Also we read in this storie—
God, in the Mownt of Synai,
75 Toke Moises these comaundmentis verelye
Wrytten with his owne hande
In tables of ston, as reade I;
But when men honoured mawmentry,
He brake them in anger hastelye,
80 For that he wold not wonde.

But afterward sone, leeve ye me,
Other tables of stone made he—
In which God bade wrytten shold be
His wordes that were before;
85 The which tables shryned were
After as God can Moyses leare.
And that shryne to them was deare
Thereafter evermore.

*Moses descends from the mountain and from another part of the mountain
comes King Balak riding.*

KING BALAACK   I, Balaack, king of Moab land,
90 All Israell I had it in my hand.
I am so wroth, I wold not wond
To slaye them, ech wighte.
For their God helpes them, stiflye

67–8. And it is still followed honestly by all who are virtuous.

69–72. If we were to undertake to play all of this story, a month would not
be long enough for it! So we shall select those subjects, as you will see, that are
most profitable.

80. Because he would not tolerate that.

85–6. These tablets were enshrined in a place which God indicated to Moses.

89. Balak, King of the Moabites, sought the help of the prophet Balaam against
the Israelites who had camped near his people. See *Numbers* 21–24.

91. I would not hesitate to kill them.

Of other landes to have mastrye,
95 That it is bootles witterlie
Against them for to fighte.

What nation soever dose them noye,
Moyses prayes anone in hye.
Therefore have they sone the victorie,
100 And other men, they have the worse.
Therfore how I will wroken be
I have bethought, as mot I the!
Balaam (I will) shall come to me,
That people for to curse:

105 For sworde ne knife may not avayle
These ilke shroes for to assaile;
That fowndes to fight he shall faile,
For sicker is hym no boote.
All nations they doe any,
110 And my selfe they can destroie,
As ox that gnawes biselie
The grasse right to the roote.

Who so Balaam blesses I wis,
Blessed sickerlie that man is;
115 Who so he curses, fareth amisse—
Such loos over all has he.
Therfore goe fetch hym, Bachler,
That he may curse the people here;
For sicker on them in no manner
120 Mon we not wroken be.

KNIGHT Syr, on your errand I will gone;
It shall be well done, and that anone.
For he shall wreak you on your fone,
The people of Israell.

---

95. It really is quite useless.

101–2. Indeed (*lit.* as I may thrive) I have thought hard and long as to how I can be revenged.

117. A bachelor-knight.

119–120. For indeed there is no other way in which we can be revenged on them.

BALAACK   125   Yea, looke thou het hym gold great wone—
                 And riches for to lyve upon,
                 To destroy them if he can—
                 The freakes that be so fell.

The Knight goes to Balaam.

KNIGHT   Balaam, my lorde greetes well thee,
           130   And prayes the right sone at hym to be,
                 To curse the people of Iudy
                 That do hym great anoye.
BALAAM   Forsooth, I tell the, Bacheler,
                 That I may have no power,
           135   But if Gods will were—
                 That shall I witt in hye.

GOD (*from above*) Balaam, I comaund the,
                 King Balaak his bydding that thou flee.
                 That people that is blessed of me,
           140   Curse thou not by no waye.
BALAAM   Lord I must doe thy byddinge—
                 Thoughe it be to me unlykeing;
                 For, truly, much wynninge
                 I might have had to-daye.

GOD   145   Thoughe the folke be my foe,
                 Thou shalt have leave thydder to goe;
                 But looke that thou doe right soe
                 As I have thee taughte.
BALAAM   Lord it shall be done in height.
           150   This asse shall beare me aright;
                 Goe we together anone, sir knight,
                 For now leave I have coughte.

They ride back to the King and Balaam speaks to the knight.

BALAAM   Now, by the law I leve upon,
                 Sith I have leave for to gone,
           155   They shal be cursed every one—

---

130. And requests you to come to him immediately (in order). . . .
135–6. Unless it be God's will – and I shall know (if that is so) at once.
147–8. But see to it that you do exactly as I have commanded you.
152. Because now I have been granted permission.

           And I ought wyn maye.
           If Balaak hold that he has heighte,
           Gods hest I set at light;
           Warryed they shal be this night,
    160   Or that I wend awaye

An angel appears before Balaam, with a drawn sword in its hand, and the ass halts.

BALAAM   Goe forth Burnell! Goe forth, goe!
               What the dyvell! My Asse will not goe.
               Served me she never soe
               What sorrow so her dose nye.

    165   Rise up, Burnell! Make thee bowne
               And helpe to beare me out the towne
               Or, as brok I my crowne,
               Thou shalt full sore abye!

Balaam beats the ass who then speaks to him.

ASS   Maister, thou dost evell witterly,
    170   So good an ass as me to nye;
               Now hast thou beaten me thry
               That beare the thus aboute.

BALAAM   Burnell, whye begiles thou me
               When I have most nede to the?

ASS   175   That sight that I before me see,
               Makes me downe to lowte.
               Am I not, master, thyne owne ass
               That ever before ready was
               To beare the whether thou woldest pas?

    180   To smyte me now, it is shame.
               Thou wottest well, master, pardy,
               Thou haddest never ass like to me,
               Ne never yet thus served I thee.
               Now I am not to blame.

Balaam now sees the Angel with a sword and, falling in a posture of worship, he says:

---

   156. If I can gain anything (by so doing).
   158. I shall pay little (or no) attention to God's prohibition.
   163-4. She has never done this to me before no matter what distress has worried her.
   176. Causes me to bend down.

BALAAM	185	Ah Lord, to thee I make avowe
		I had no sight of thee erre now;
		Lyttle wist I it was thou
		That feared my asse soe.
ANGEL		Why hast thou beaten thy ass thry?
	190	Now I am comen thee to nye
		That changes thy purpose falcelye
		And woldest be my foe.
		And the ass had not downe gone,
		I wold have slayne thee here anone.
BALAAM	195	Lord, have pittye me upon,
		For sinned I have sore.
		Is it thy will that I forth goe?
ANGEL		Yea, but looke thou doe this folk no woe
		Otherwise then God bade thee tho,
	200	And saide to thee before.

Balaam and the knight go forward and Balak enters from the other side to meet them.

BALAACK		Ah! welcome, Balaam my frend,
		For all myne anguish thou shalt end,
		If that thy will be to wend
		And wreake me of my foe.
BALAAM (*aside to the audience*)		Nought may I speake, so have I win,
		But as God puttes me in
		To forby all and my kin.
		Therfore, sure me is woe.
BALAACK		Com forth, Balaam, come with me!
	210	For on this hill, so mot I thee,
		The folke of Israell thou shalt see—
		And curse them, I thee praye.
		Thou shalt have riches, golde, and fee,
		And I shall advance thy dignytye;

---

190. I am now come to trouble you.
205–8. As I hope for joy (in Heaven) I can say nothing except what God tells me to, in order to save everything (I possess) and my family. For this reason I am bound to suffer.

215   To curse men, cursed they may be,
       That thou shalt see to day.

Balaam is led on to a mountain and, looking to the south, he says:

BALAAM   How may I curse them in this place—
       The people that God blessed hase?
       In them is both might and grace,
220   And that is always seene.
       Wytnes I may none beare
       Against God, that this can were
       His people, that no man may deare
       Ne troble with no teene.

225   I saye these folkes shall have their will:
       That no nation shall them gryll.
       The goodnes that they shall fulfill
       Nombred may not be.
       Their God shall them kepe and save.
230   No other represe may I not have;
       But such death as they shall have
       I praye God send me.

BALAACK   What the Devilles eyles the, poplart!
       Thy speach is not worth a fart;
235   Doted I wot well thou art,
       For woodlie thou hast wrougt.
       I bade thee curse them, every one,
       And thou blest them, blood and bone;
       To this North syde thou shalt anon,
240   For here thy deed is nought.

Balaam is now taken to the north side of the stage.

BALAAM   Herken Balaack what I say:
       God may not gibb by no waye.
       That he saith, is veray,

---

215. If you curse them, they will be cursed.

221–4. I cannot bear witness against God who can defend his people against this (my curse), so that no one can injure or vex them.

230. I shall not lay myself open to a second reproof (from God).

235–6. Now I know you are off your head, for you have acted like a madman.

240. For your (blessing) is null and void (in this north side).

For he may not lye.
245 To bless his folk he me sent;
Therfore I saie, as I am kent,
That in this land, verament,
Is used no mawmentry.

To Jacobs blood and Israell
250 God shall send joy and heale;
And, as a lyon in his weale,
Christ shal be haunsed hye
And rise also, in noble araye,
As a prynce to wyn great paye,
255 Overcome his enemyes, as I say,
And them bowndly bye.

BALAACK   What the Devill is this? Thou cursest them naught,
Nor blessest them nether, as me thought.
BALAAM   Syr kinge, this I thee beheight,
260 Or that I come here.
BALAACK   Yet shalt thou to another place,
Ther Gods power for to embrace.
The Dyvell geve the hard grace,
But thou doe my prayer!   *Goes to the east side.*

BALAAM   265 Ah Lord, that here is fayre wonning,
Halls, chambers of great lyking,
Valleyes, woodes, grass springing,
Fayre yordes, and eke rivers—
I wot well God made all this,
270 His folke to lyve in joye and blisse.
That warryeth them warried is,
That blessest them to God is deare.

---

246. For this reason I say, as I have been instructed (by God).

251. The dramatist here echoes *Numbers* 23: 24 and, more particularly, *Numbers* 24: 9.

256. And easily redeem them (the children of Israel).

263–4. May the Devil deal harshly with you unless you do as I ask.

271–2. Whoever injures them is accursed and whoever blesses them is dear to God.

BALAACK		Popelard, thou preachest as a pie.
		The devill of hell thee destroy!
	275	I bade thee curse myne enemye,
		Therfore thou came me to;
		Now hast thou blessed them here thry—
		For the nones me to nye.
BALAAM		So tould I the before, twye—
	280	I might none other doe.
BALAACK		Out! alas! What dyvell ayles thee?
		I have het thee gold and fee,
		To speake but wordes two or three;
		And thou makes much distance.
	285	Yet once I will assay thee
		If any boote of bale will be;
		And, if thou falcely now faile me,
		Mahound geve thee mischance!

Now, looking upwards to heaven, Balaam prophesies.

BALAAM		Now, one thinge I will tell you all—
	290	Hereafter what shall befall:
		A starre of Jacob springe shall,
		A man of Israell;
		He shall overcome, and have in band,
		All kinges, dukes of strang land,
	295	And all the world have in his hand—
		As lord to dight and deale.

Enter various Old Testament prophets in procession.

ISAIAH		I saye a mayden meeke and mylde
		Shall conceave and beare a childe,
		Cleane without workes wilde,
	300	To wyn mankinde to wayle.

277–8. Each time you have blessed them (and not cursed them) in order to anger me.

284–6. You are causing a great deal of trouble. I shall try once again to see if you will amend your wrong-doing.

296. As their sovereign, to rule and control.

297. The biblical references for this and the succeeding prophecies of Christ's advent are *Isaiah* 7: 14–16; *Ezekiel* 44: 2, 3; *Jeremiah* 14: 17; *Jonah* 2: 2–10; *Psalm* 18; *Joel* 2: 28–29; *Micah* 5: 2.

Butter and hony shall be his meate,
That he may all evill foryeat,
Our soules out of hell to get—
And called Emanuell.

On the side of the stage.

EXPOSITOR 305 Lordinges, these wordes are so veray
That exposition, in good faye,
None needes, but you know may
This word 'Emanuell'.
'Emanuell' is as much to saye
310 As, 'God with us night and day';
Therfore, that name for ever and aye
To his sonne cordes wondrous well.

EZEKIEL I Ezechiell, sothlie see
A gate in Gods house on hye;
315 Closed it was, no man came nye.
Then told an angell me:
'This gate shall no man open, I wis,
For god will come and goe by this;
For himself it reserved is—
320 None shall come there but hee.'

EXPOSITOR By this gate, lords—verament
I understand in my intent—
That way the holy ghost in went,
When God tooke flesh and bloode
325 In that sweet mayden Mary.
Shee was that gate wytterly,
For in her he light graciouslie—
Mankind to doe good.

JEREMIAH My eyes must run and sorrow, aye
330 Without ceasing, night and daye,
For my daughter, soth to saye,

307-8. Except that you may wish to know the meaning of this word 'Emanuel'.

311-12. That name agrees precisely and exactly with God's son.

321-2. Truly, the way I interpret it is this.

327. For he took up his abode graciously in her.

Shall suffer great anye.
And my folke shall doe, in faye,
Thinges that they ne know may
335 To that mayden, by many waye,
And her sonne, sickerlie.

EXPOSITOR Lordinges, this prophesie, I wis,
Touches the Passion, nothing amisse;
For the prophet see well this
340 What shall come—as I reade—
That a childe, borne of a maye,
Shall suffer death, sooth to saye,
And they that mayden shall afray—
Have vengeance for that deede.

JONAH 345 I Jonas, in full great any
To God I prayed inwardlie;
And he me hard through his mercy,
And on me did his grace.
In myddes the sea cast was I—
350 For I wrought inobedyentlie—
But in a whalles bellye
Three dayes saved I was.

EXPOSITOR Lordinges, what this may signifie
Christ expoundes apertelie,
355 As we reade in the Evangely,
That Christ himself can saie:
Right as Jonas was dayes three
In wombe of whall, so shall he be
In earth lyinge—as was he—
360 And rise the third daye.

DAVID I Davyd, saie that God almighte
From ye highest heaven to earth will light,
And thidder againe with full might—
Both God and man in feare—
365 And after come to deeme the righte.

333-6. Believe me, my people shall, in different ways, act towards that virgin and her son in ignorance of what they do.
338. Clearly concerns the Passion.

May no man shape them of his sight
Ne deeme that to mankind is dighte—
But all then must apeare.

EXPOSITOR   Lordes, this speach is so veray,
370 That to expound it to your paye,
It needes nothing, in good faye—
This speach is so expresse.
Each man by it knowe may
That of the Ascention, soth to saie,
375 David prophesied in his daye,
As yt rehearsed was.

JOEL   I Joell, saie this sickerlye,
That my ghost send will I
Upon mankinde, merciably
380 From heaven, sitting in see;
Then shold our childer prophesie,
Ould men meet sweens wytterly;
Yong se sightes that therby
Many wise shall be.

EXPOSITOR   385 Lordinges, this prophet speakes here,
In Gods person as it were,
And prophesies that he will apeare
Ghostlie to mankinde;
This signes non other, in good faye,
390 But of his deede on Whitsonday—
Sending his ghost, that we ever may
On hym have sadlie mynd.

MICAH   I Micheas, through my mynde
Will saye that man shall sothlie finde
395 That a Childe of kinges kinde

366-7. No man can hide himself from God's sight nor decide what is to happen to mankind.

383-4. Young men shall see visions that will bring wisdom to many.

391-2. So that we should always think steadfastly on him.

395. Of royal blood.

In Bethlem shall be borne,
That shall be duke to dight and deale,
And rule the folke of Israell;
Also wyn againe mankindes heale
400 That, through Adam, was lorne.

EXPOSITOR   Lordinges, two thinges apertlie
You may see in this prophesie;
The place certefies thee, sothlie,
Where Christ borne will be;
405 And after his ending, sickerlie,
Of his deedes of great mercy,
That he shold sit soveraynly
In heaven, thereas is he.

Moe prophetis, lordinges, we might play,
410 But it wold tary much the daye;
Therfore six, sothe to say,
Are played in this place.
Twoo speakes of his Incarnation,
An other of Christs Passion,
415 The fourth of the Resurrection.
In figure of Jonas.

The fifte speakes expreslie
How he, from the highest heaven hye,
Light into earth, us to forby,
420 And after thydder steigh
With oure kinde to heaven blisse.
More love might he not shew, I wis;
But right there as hym selfe is
He haunshed our kinde on high.

425 The sixt shewes, you may see,
His Goste to man send will he,

399–400. And also to gain back for mankind that happiness (state of health)
that was lost through Adam.
406. Because of his deeds.
408. Where he now is.
420–1. And later ascended there to the joy of heaven with our nature.
423–4. He exalted our human nature so that it enjoys a status (or a place) by
His own side.

More stidfast that they shal be
To love God evermore.
Thus that beleven, that leven we,
430   Of Gods deedes that had pittye
One man, when that he made them free,
Is prophesied here before.

BALAACK   Goe we forth! It is no boote
Longer with this man to moote.
435   For God of Jewes is crop and roote—
And lord of heaven and hell.
Now see I well; no man on lyve
Gaynes with him for to stryve.
Therefore here, as mot I thryve,
440   I will no longer dwell.   *Exit.*

EXPOSITOR   Lordinges, much more matter
Is in this story then you see here,
But the substance, without were,
Is played you beforne.
445   And by these prophesies, leav you me,
Three kinges, as you shall played see,
Presented at his nativitye
Christ, when he was borne.

The end of the Fifth Pageant.

---

427. So that they shall love God more steadfastly evermore.
429–432. Thus that article of faith, in which we believe, concerning God's
actions when he took pity on man by releasing him from sin, is here prophesied.
435. Is the beginning and end (Alpha and omega).
445. Believe you me.

V. The Annunciation

The Annunciation is the twelfth of the forty-eight pageants that comprise the York Cycle of Mystery Plays. This pageant was produced by *The Spicers*—which is its title in the *Ashburnham Manuscript*—the only extant version of the cycle of plays. This manuscript seems to have been a 'fair copy' made for official purposes and the manuscript (which was probably written late in the fifteenth century) indicates that some of the plays had been composed afresh (*de novo*) for this copy. The play is written in the Northern dialect; the stage directions are editorial. A shortened version of the cycle of plays was successfully performed in modern English at York in 1951, and, since then, every three years. (See Bibliography under *J. S. Purvis*.)
MS: British Museum, Additional 35290.

Doctor   Mary   Angel   Elizabeth

DOCTOR
Lord God, grete mervell es to mene
Howe man was made with-outen mysse
And sette whare he sulde ever have bene—
With-outen bale, bidand in blisse.

5 And howe he lost that comforth clene,
And was putte oute fro Paradys,
And, sithen, what sorouse sor warre sene
Sente un-to hym and to al his;
And howe they lay lange space

10 In helle, lokyn fro lyght,
Tille God graunted tham grace
Of helpe als he hadde hyght.

Than is it nedfull for to neven,
How prophettis all Goddis counsailes kende,

15 Als prophet Amos in his steven,

---

1. The Latin heading above the play reads: 'A Doctor explains the sayings of the Prophets about Christ's Nativity. Mary, the Angel greets her, Mary greets Elizabeth.' A later marginal note in English reads, 'Doctor, this matter is newly made, wherof we have no coppy.' The entire Prologue, then, was spoken by an actor dressed as a Doctor of Divinity.

5. 'The sheer joy' of 'blisse', i.e. the Earthly Paradise before the Fall.

7–8. And afterwards what bitter sorrows were obviously (? as we know) sent to (afflict) man and all that belong to him.

Lered whils he in his liffe gan lende.
He sais thus: God the Fadir in heven
Ordand in erthe man kynde to mende;
And to grayth it with godhede even,
20   His sone, he saide, that he suld sende
To take kynde of man-kyn
In a mayden full mylde.
So was many saved of syn
And the foule fende be-gyled.

25   And for the feende suld so be fedd
Be tyne and to no treuth take tentt,
God made that mayden to be wedded
Or he his sone unto hir sentte.
So was the godhede closed and cledde
30   In wede of weddyng whare thy wente;
And that oure blysse sulde so be bredde,
Ful many materes may be mente.
God hym self sayde this thynge
To Abraham, als hym liste:
35   Of thy sede sall uppe sprynge
Whare in folke sall be bliste.

To prove thes prophettes ordande er—
Als I say un-to olde and yenge—
He moved oure myscheves for to merr;
40   For thus he prayed God for this thynge:
Lord, late thou doune, at thy likyng,
The dewe to fall fro heven so ferre;
For than the erthe sall sprede and sprynge
A seede, that us sall save

---

16. Taught as long as his life lasted.

18. Decreed that man's lot on earth should be improved.

25–6. And in order that the Devil should be filled with vexation and yet be
unable to see the truth (of God's true purposes).

29–30. Enclosed and dressed in the robes of wedlock.

37. Here is the proof that these prophets were inspired (to forecast Christ's
birth). The Doctor, like the Expositor in the Chester plays, wishes to show the
essential unity of purpose that underlies the pageants.

39. He acted in order to put an end to our wrong doings.

45   That nowe in blisse are bente.
Of clerkis who-so will crave
Thus may ther 'gratis' be mente.

The dewe to the gode Halygaste
May be remeved in mannes mynde;
50   The erthe unto the mayden chaste
Bycause sho comes of erthely kynde.
Thir wise wordis ware noght wroght in waste
To waffe and wende away als wynde;
For this same prophett sone in haste
55   Saide, forthermore, als folkes may fynde.
Loo, he sais thus, God sall gyffe
Here-of a syngne to see
Tille all that lely lyffe,
And this thare sygne sal be.

60   Loo! he sais, a mayden mon
Here, on this molde, mankynde omell,
Ful clere consayve and bere a sonne,
And neven his name Emanuell.
His kyngdom that ever is begonne,
65   Sall never sese but dure and dwell;
On David sege, thore sall he wonne,
His domes to deme and trueth to telle.
He says, luffe of oure Lorde
All this sall ordan thanne,
70   That mennes pees and accorde
To make with erthely manne.

More of this maiden me meves he,
This prophett sais for oure socoure:

46-7. If any one were to ask the scholars they would say that we should interpret this (i.e. the reference to 'dew' in l. 42 and in Isaac's blessing in *Genesis* 27: 27-9) as referring to grace (*gratis*).

48-50. In human terms the dew stands for the (good) Holy Spirit and the earth for the pure virgin.

58. To all who live virtuously (i.e. loyally according to God's law).

66-7. He shall occupy David's throne in order to give his judgement. . . .

68-71. Love of our Lord shall so bring this about that on earth men shall live in peace and harmony together.

72-3. The prophet says many other things about this virgin, for our comfort.

A wande sall brede of Jesse boure;
75   And of this same also, sais hee,
Uponne that wande sall springe a floure
Wher-on the Haly Gast sall be,
To governe it with grete honnoure.
That wande meynes untill us
80   This mayden, even and morne;
And the floure is Jesus,
That of that blyst bees borne.

The prophet Johell, a gentill Jewe,
Som-tyme has saide of the same thyng?:
85   He likenes Criste, even als he knewe,
Like to the dewe in doune commyng.
The maiden of Israell al newe,
He sais, sall bere one and forthe brynge,
Als the lelly floure full faire of hewe—
90   This meynes sa, to olde and yenge,
That the hegh Haly Gaste,
Come oure myscheffe to mende,
In Marie mayden chaste,
When God his sone walde sende.

95   This lady is to the lilly lyke—
That is, bycause of hir clene liffe;
For in this worlde was never slyke
One to be mayden, modir, and wyffe,
And hir sonne kyng in heven-ryke—
100 Als oft es red be reasoune ryfe—
And hir husband, bath maistir and meke,
In charite to stynte all striffe.

---

80. 'Even and morne'—a rhyming tag = 'at all times'.
82. Who is born of that Blessed One.
86. To the dew as it falls. (Cf. *Joel* 2: 18–29.)
93–4. When God should send his son to live in Mary, the pure virgin.
97–8. For never in this world has there been such a one that was virgin, mother and wife.
100. As is frequently made clear (? interpreted) by numerous arguments.

This passed all worldly witte:
How God had ordand thaim thanne,
105 In hir one to be knytte—
Godhed, maydenhed, and manne.

Bot of this werke grete witnes was
With forme-faders, all folke may tell.
Whan Jacob blyst his sone Judas,
110 He told the tale thaim two emell;
He sais, the septer sall noght passe
Fra Juda lande of Israell,
Or he comme that God ordand has
To be sente, feendis force to fell.
115 Hym sall alle folke abyde,
And stande un-to his steven;
Ther sawes wer signified
To Crist, Goddis sone in heven.

For howe he was sente, se we more,
120 And howe God wolde his place purvay;
He saide: 'Sonne, I sall sende by-fore
Myne aungell to rede the thy way.'
Of John Baptist he menyd thore—
For in erthe he was ordand, ay
125 To warne the folke that wilsom wore
Of Cristis comyng, and thus gon say:
'Eftir me sall come nowe
A man of myghtost mast,
And sall baptis yowe
130 In the high Haly Gast.'

103–5. This has surpassed all human comprehension: how God has contrived
to unite all three states in one (woman).

109–14. For Jacob's blessing bestowed on Judah, see *Genesis* 49:8–12. The
original tribal history of Judah, especially important because Jesus was born in
Judaea, is given in *Genesis* 38.

113–14. Before he comes whom God has ordained to put an end to the
power of the fiend.

117. All their (the Prophet's) sayings pointed towards.

119. We shall see later how he was sent (to earth).

126–30. See *Matthew* 3:11.

128. A man who is the greatest of all mighty ones.

> Thus, of Cristis commyng, may we see
> How sainte Luke spekis in his gospell:
> Fro God in heven es sent, sais he,
> An aungell is named Gabriell
> 135   To Nazareth in Galale,
> Where than a mayden mylde gon dwell,
> That with Joseph suld wedded be.
> Hir name is Marie; thus gan he telle,
> To God his grace than grayd
> 140   To man in this manere—
> And how the aungell saide
> Takes hede, all that will here.

Then the angel appears and sings.

ANGEL   Hayle! Marie! full of grace and blysse!
        Oure Lord God is with the,
145   And has chosen the for his;
        Of all women blist mot thou be.

MARY   What maner of halsyng is this
        Thus prevely comes to me;
        For in myn herte a thoght it is,
150   The tokenyng that I here see.

        The angel sings; Mary is afraid.

ANGEL   Ne drede the noght, thou mylde Marie,
        For no-thyng that may befalle;
        For thou has fun soveranly
        At God a grace over othir all.
155   In chastite of thy bodye
        Consayve and bere a childe thou sall;
        This bodword brynge I the forthy—
        His name Jesu sall thou calle.

        Mekill of myght than sall he bee,
160   He sall be God and called God sonne.

---

132. See *Luke* 1: 26–80 which is the basis of the following action.

138–40. In this way he fore-tells how God prepared his grace for mankind in a (special) manner.

153–4. For you have received from God a sovereign favour above all other women.

159. He shall become all-powerful.

David sege, his fadir free,
Sall God hym giffe to sytte uppon;
Als kyng for ever regne sall hee,
In Jacob house ay for to wonne.

165 Of his kyngdome and dignite
Shall noo man erthly knaw ne con.

MARY Thou Goddis aungell, meke and mylde,
Howe sulde it be, I the praye,
That I sulde consayve a childe
170 Of any man by nyght or daye.
I knawe no man that shulde have fyled
My maydenhode, the sothe to saye.
Withouten will of werkis wilde,
In chastite I have ben ay.

ANGEL 175 The Halygast in the sall lighte,
Hegh vertue sall to the holde;
The holy birthe of the so bright,
God sonne he sall be calde.
Loo, Elyzabeth thi cosyne ne myght
180 In elde consayve a childe for alde—
This is the sexte moneth, full ryght,
To hir that baran has ben talde.

MARY Thou aungell, blissid messanger,
Of Goddis will I holde me payde;
185 I love my lorde with herte dere,
The grace that he has for me layde.
Goddis handmayden, lo! me here,
To his wille all redy grayd;
Be done to me of all manere,
190 Thurgh thy worde als thou hast saide.

165-6. No mortal man can know or comprehend the extent of his kingdom and authority.

173. Without any inclination for passionate acts.

176. Virtue from on high shall be joined to you.

177-8. Your holy and radiant off-spring shall be called the son of God.

181-2. She, who had been considered barren, is exactly six months with child.

184. I am pleased to do God's will.

189-190. Let everything be done to me exactly as you have said.

ANGEL   Now God, that all oure hope is in,
                        Thurgh the myght of the Haly Gaste,
                        Save the, dame, fro sak of synne,
                        And wisse the fro all werkis wast!   *Exit.*

Mary visits her cousin Elizabeth.

MARY   195   Elyzabeth, myn awne cosyne,
                        Me thoght I coveyte alway mast
                        To speke with the of all my kynne;
                        Therfore I comme thus in this hast.

ELIZABETH   Welcome! mylde Marie,
               200   Myne aughen cosyne so dere.
                        Joifull woman am I,
                        That I nowe see the here.
                        Blissid be thou anely
                        Of all women in feere,
               205   And the frute of thy body
                        Be blissid, ferre and nere.

                        This is joyfull tydyng
                        That I may nowe here see—
                        The modyr of my lord kyng,
               210   Thus-gate come to me.
                        Sone als the voyce of thine haylsing
                        Moght myn neres entre and be,
                        The childe in my wombe so yenge
                        Makes grete myrthe unto the.

MARY   215   Nowe lorde, blist be thou ay
                        For the grace thou has me lente.
                        Lorde I lofe the, God verray,
                        The sande thou hast me sente.
                        I thanke the nyght and day,
               220   And prayes, with goode entente,
                        Thou make me to thy paye—
                        To the my wille is wentte.

---

194. And direct you away from all wasteful deeds.

211–14. As soon as the sound of your voice in greeting had entered and
stayed in my ears, the young child in my womb gave signs of joy towards you.

ELIZABETH   Blissid be thou, grathely grayed
                 To God thurgh chastite;
       225   Thou trowed and helde the payed
                 Atte his wille for to bee.
                 All that to the is saide
                 Fro my lorde so free,
                 Swilke grace is for the layde,
       230   Sall be fulfilled in the.

MARY   To his grace I will me ta
                 With chastite to dele,
                 That made me thus to ga
                 Omange his maidens feele.
       235   My saule sall lovying ma
                 Unto that lorde so lele,
                 And my gast make joye alswa
                 In God that es my hele.   *She sings the 'Magnificat'*

                         FINIS

In the *York Cycle* there follows the pageant about 'Joseph's trouble about
Mary,' performed by *The Pewterers and Foundours.*

---

225. You believed and held yourself in readiness to do his will.
229. Such grace is prepared for you (and shall be . . .).
235-6. My soul shall sing praise unto the true Lord.

VI. Herod and the Slaying of the Innocents

Only two plays from the authentic Coventry Cycle have survived into modern times. The following play is the second half of the pageant presented by the *Shearmen and Taylors;* the first half describes the Annunciation and Nativity of Jesus, the visit of the shepherds to the manger, and a fairly long discussion between 'two prophets' which interprets the significance of the birth of Christ. As they leave the stage, our portion of the play begins. ('There the profettis gothe furthe and Erod cumyth in, and the messenger.') There is no extant manuscript and the following text is based on the two versions printed (from a now missing manuscript) by Thomas Sharp in his *Illustrative Papers of the History of Coventry* (limited edition, 1817) and his *A Dissertation on the Coventry Mysteries* (1825). The latter contains a great deal of information derived from local Coventry records which date from the late sixteenth century and suggest that the original cycle belonged to the first quarter of the previous century.

Enter Herod and the Herald.

HERALD   Faytes pais, dñyis, baronys de grande reynownc!
        Payis, seneoris, schevaleris de nooble posance!
        Pays, gentis homos, companeonys petis egrance!
        Je vos command dugard treytus sylance.
    5 Payis, tanque vottur nooble Roie syre ese presance!
        Que nollis persone ese non fawis perwynt dedfferance,
        Nese harde de frappas; mayis gardus to to paceance,—
        Mayis gardus voter seneor to cor reyuerance;
        Car elat vottur Roie to to puysance.

1–11. The herald speaks a corrupt form of (official) Anglo-French and addresses the audience like a royal herald preparing the populace for a king's entry. Roughly translated as 'Pray silence, my lords, barons of great renown! Silence, noble sirs, Knights of noble rank and authority! Silence, gentlemen, companions of all kinds! (lit. small and great, major and minor orders(?)). I command you all to maintain the most absolute silence! Silence, as long as your noble sire, the King, is present! so that no person here present will diminish one jot of reverence nor be so bold as to applaud, but maintain a (complete) attitude of complete deference. Rather show due heartfelt reverence to your Seigneur. For he is your all-powerful King. In his name, all be silent! I command you. And may the devil himself take you off, O King Herod.' This last sentence is an aside to the audience.

10   Anon de leo, pase tos! je vose cummande,
      E lay Roie erott, la grandeaboly vos vmport.

HEROD   Qui statis in Jude et Rex Iseraell,
         And the myghttyst conquerowre that ever walkid
             on grownd;
         For I am evyn he thatt made bothe hevin and hell,
15   And of my myghte powar holdith vp this world
             rownd.
         Magog and Madroke, bothe the[m] did I con-
             fownde,
         And, with this bryght bronde, there bonis I brak
             onsunder,
         Thatt all the wyde worlde on those rappis did
             wonder.
         I am the caws of this grett lyght and thunder;
20   Ytt ys throgh my fure that the soche noyse dothe
             make.
         My feyrefull contenance the clowdis so doth in-
             cumbur
         That oftymis, for drede ther-of, the verre yerth
             doth quake.
         Loke, when I, with males, this bryght brond doth
             schake,
         All the whole worlde from the north to the sowthe,
25   I ma them dystroie with won worde of my mowthe.

         To reycownt vnto you myn inneumerabull sub-
             stance
         Thatt were to moche for any tong to tell;

---

12. Herod carries on this mock-solemn mood by beginning to introduce
himself in Latin.

16. Magog and Madroke are presented by our dramatist as powerful and
malevolent monarchs on the borders of Israel who were overthrown by Herod
the Great—one of three Herods named in the N.T.—who was appointed
King of the Jews by the Romans and ruled from 37–4 B.C. There are three
references to Magog in *Ezekiel* 38, 39, *Genesis* 10:2, and *Revelation* 20:8.
Madroke appears to be a conflation of the names Meshech and Madai which,
on different occasions, are associated with Magog.

20. It is because of my fury that you (i.e. the thunder and lightning which
accompanied his speech) make such a noise.

For all the whole Orent ys under myn obbeydeance,
And prynce am I of Purgatorre, and cheff capten of
    hell;

30 And those tyraneos trayturs be force ma I compell
Myne enmyis to vanquesse and evyn to dust them
    dryve,
And with a twynke of myn iee, not won to be lafte
    alyve.
Behald my contenance and my colur,
Bryghtur then the sun in the meddis of the dey;
35 Where can you have a more grettur succur,
Then to behold my person that ys soo gaye?
My fawcun and my fassion, with my gorgis araye,—
He thatt had the grace all-wey ther-on to thynke,
Lyve he myght all-wey with-owt othur meyte or
    drynke.

40 And thys my tryumfande fame most hylist dothe
    abownde
Throgh-owt this world, in all reygeons abrod,
Reysemelyng the faver of thatt most myght
    Mahownd;
From Jubytor be desent and cosyn to the grett God,
And namyd the most reydowndid kyng Eyrodde,
45 Wyche thatt all pryncis hath under subjeccion
And all there whole powar undur my proteccion.
And therefore, my hareode here, callid Calcas,
Warne thow eyvere porte, thatt noo schyppis aryve,
Nor also aleond stranger throg my realme pas—
50 But the for there truage do pay markis fyve.
Now spede the forth hastele,
For the thatt wyll the contrare,
Apon a galowse hangid schal be,
And, be Mahownde, of me the gett noo grace.

HERALD   55 Now, lord and mastur, in all the hast
Thy worethe wyll ytt schall be wroght;

---

32. And to kill them all with one glance of my eye.
50. Unless they pay five marks as tribute.

And thy ryall cuntreyis schal be past
In asse schort tyme ase can be thoght.

HEROD   Now schall owre regeons throgh-owt be soght
60   In eyvere place, bothe est and west;
Yff any katyffis to me be broght,
Yt schal be nothyng for there best.
And the whyle thatt I do resst,
Trompettis, viallis, and othur armone
65   Schall bles the wakyng of my majeste.

Here Erod goth awey and the iij kyngis speykyth in the strete.
1ST KING   Now blessid be God of his swet sonde,
For yondur a feyre bryght star I do see!
Now ys he comon us a-monge,
Asse the profettis seyd thatt yt schuld be.
70   A seyd there schuld a babe be borne,
Comyng of the rote of Jesse,
To sawe mankynd that wasse for-lorne;
And truly comen now ys he.

Reyverence and worschip to hym woll I do,
75   Asse God and man thatt all made of noght.
All the profettis acordid, and seyd evyn soo,
That with hys presseos blod mankynd schuld be
boght.
He grant me grace, be yonder star that I see,
And into thatt place bryng me,
80   Thatt I ma hym worschipe with umellete
And se hys gloreose face.

2ND KING   Owt of my wey I deme thatt I am,
For toocuns of thys cuntrey can I non see;
Now God, thatt on yorth madist man,
85   Send me sum knoleyge where thatt I be.
Yondur, me thynke, a feyre bryght star I see,
The wyche betocunyth the byrth of a chyld

---

57. And (messengers) shall traverse your royal domains. . . .
59. Now our country shall be thoroughly searched.
75. As both God and man who created everything out of nothing.

Thatt hedur ys cum to make man fre—
He borne of a mayde, and sche nothyng defyld.

90   To worschip thatt chyld ys myn intent;
Forth now wyll I take my wey.
I trust sum cumpany God hathe me sent,
For yonder I see a kyng labur on the wey;
Towarde hym now woll I ryde.

95   Harke, cumly kyng, I you pray,
Into whatt cost wyll ye thys tyde,
Or weddur lyis youre jurney?

1ST KING   To seke a chylde ys myne intent
Of whom the profetis hathe ment;

100 The tyme ys cum; now ys he sent;
Be yondur star here ma you see.

2ND KING   Sir, I prey you, with your lysence,
To ryde with you unto his presence;
To hym wyll I offur frank-in-sence,

105 For the hed of all Whole Churche schall he be.

3RD KING   I ryde wanderyng in veyis wyde
Over montens and dalis; I wot not where I am.
Now, Kyng of all kyngis, send me soche gyde
Thatt I myght have knoleyge of thys cuntreys
name.

110 Ayondur I se a syght, besemyng all afar,
The wyche betocuns sum neuis, ase I troo;

---

89. He, born of a virgin, and she in no way defiled.

96. To what district (country?) are you going at this time.

104. Medieval tradition—which also connected the three Kings with the descendants of Balaam—developed a complex series of allegorical significances around the three gifts of the Magi. (Cf. *A Stanzaic Life of Christ*, edited by F. A. Foster, *E.E.T.S.* 166, pp. 68–70.) By custom in those days gifts were brought to God or a King: the gold helped to relieve Mary's poverty, the frankincense purified the stench in the stable, the myrrh was used to annoint the child's limbs. Further, gold signified a King, incense a bishop, and myrrh Christ's burial. Finally, the gold implied love, incense devotion, and myrrh a symbol of mastery over the flesh.

105. For He shall be the head of the Holy Catholic Church.

110–111. Over there I perceive a vision—as though it came from afar, which signifies some new tidings (event), as I believe.

        Asse me thynke, a chyld peryng in a stare.

        I trust he be cum that schall defend us from woo.

        To kyngis yondur I see, and to them woll I ryde

115   For to have there cumpane; I trust the wyll me abyde.

        Hayle, cumly kyngis augent!

        Good surs, I pray you, whedder ar ye ment?

1ST KING   To seke a chylde ys owre intent,

        Wyche betocuns yonder star, asse ye ma see.

2ND KING 120 To hym I purpose thys present.

3RD KING   Surs, I pray you, and thatt ryght umblee,

        With you thatt I ma ryde in cumpane.

        To allmyghte God now prey we

        Thatt hys pressiose persone we ma se.

Here Erode cumyth in ageyne and the messenger seyth:

HERALD 125 Hayle, lorde, most off myght.

        Thy commandement ys right.

        Into thy land ys comyn this nyght

        iij kyngis and with them a grett cumpany

HEROD   Whatt make those kyngis in this cuntrey?

HERALD 130 To seke a kyng and a chyld, the sey.

HEROD   Of whatt age schuld he bee?

HERALD   Skant twellve deyis old fulle.

HEROD   And wasse he soo late borne?

HERALD   E! syr, soo the schode me: thys same dey in the morne.

HEROD 135 Now, in payne of deyth, bryng them me beforne;

        And there-fore, harrode, now hy the in hast,

        In all spede thatt thow were dyght,

        Or thatt those kyngis the cuntrey be past.

        Loke thow bryng them all iij before my syght,

---

117. Where do you intend to go?

129. What do these kings want in this land?

134. Indeed, Sir; as they told me: that very morning. According to the tradition retained in *A Stanzaic Life of Christ*, the Magi arrived in Jerusalem on the thirteenth day after they had first seen the star. The herald bases his guess at Christ's age on their information (*so the schode me*).

137–8. Make all the speed that you can before these kings have passed through my land.

140   And in Jerusalem inquere more of that chyld.
But I warne the, that thy wordis be mylde,
For there must thow hede and crafte weylde
How to fordo his powere; and those iij kyngis shal
     be begild.

HERALD   Lorde, I am redde att youre byddyng
145   To sarve the ase my lord and kyng;
For joye there-of, loo, how I spryng
With lyght hart and fresche gamboldyng
Alofte here on this molde!

HEROD   Then sped the forthe hastely,
150   And loke that thow beyre the eyvinly;
And also I pray the hartely
Thatt thow doo comand me
Bothe to yong and olde.

The messenger goes across the playing area to meet the kings.

HERALD   Hayle, syr kyngis, in youre degre.
155   Erood, kyng of these cuntreyis wyde,
Desyrith to speyke with you all thre,
And for youre comyng he dothe abyde.

1ST KING   Syr, att his wyll we be ryght bayne.
Hy us, brethur, unto thatt lordis place—
160   To speyke with hym we wold be fayne.
Thatt chyld thatt we seke, he grant us of his grace!

They move across stage to Herod.

HERALD   Hayle, lorde withowt pere!
These iij kyngis here have we broght.

HEROD   Now welcum, syr kyngis, all in fere;
165   But of my bryght ble, surs, bassche ye noght!
Sir kyngis, ase I undurstand,
A star hathe gydid you into my land—

142-3. For, there, you must exercise care and cunning in order to destroy his power.

150. And see to it that you behave discreetly.

165. Don't be amazed at my splendid appearance.

Wherein grett harie ye have fonde—
Be reysun of hir beymis bryght.
170   Wherefore I pray you hartely
The vere truthe thatt ye wold sertefy—
How long yt ys surely
Syn of that star you had furst syght.

IST KING   Sir kynge, the vere truthe to sey
175   And for to schoo you ase hit ys best—
This same ys evin the xijth dey
Syth yt aperid to us to be west.

HEROD   Brethur, then ys there no more to sey;
But with hart and wyll kepe ye your jurney
180   And cum whom by me this same wey,
Of your neuis thatt I myght knoo.
You scall tryomfe in this cuntre
And, with grett conquorde, bankett with me,
And thatt chyld myself, then, woll I see
185   And honor hym also.

2ND KING   Sir, youre commandement we woll fullfyll
And humbly abaye owreself theretyll.
He, thatt weldith all thyng at wyll,
The redde way hus teyche,
190   Sir kyng, thatt we ma passe your land in pes!

HEROD   Yes, and walke softely eyvin at your one es;
Youre paseporte for a C deyis
Here schall you have of clere cummand:
Owre reme to labur any weyis
195   Here schall you have, be spesschall grante.

3RD KING   Now farewell, kyng of hy degre;
Humbly of you owre leyve we take.

HEROD   Then adeu, Sir kyngis all thre;

_____

168. In which you have found a great deal of stir and bustle.
177. Since it appeared to us in the West.
180-1. And return back to me this same way and inform me of your news.
188-90. May He, that commands all things as he pleases, show us the proper way, your majesty, so that we may pass over your land in peace.

And whyle I lyve be bold of me!
200   There is nothyng in this cuntre
But for youre one ye schall yt take.

Exeunt Three Kings.

Now these iij kyngis are gon on ther wey
Onwysely and onwyttely have the all wroghte.
When the cum ageyne, the schall dy that same dey,
205   And thus these vyle wreychis to deyth the schal be broght—
Soche ys my lykyng.
He that against my lawis wyll hold,
Be he kyng or keysar neyver soo bold,
I schall them cast into caris cold
210   And to deyth I schall them bryng.

There Erode goth his weyis and the iij kyngis cum in ageyne.

1ST KING   O blessid God, moche ys thy myght!
                Where ys this star thatt gawe us lyght?

2ND KING   Now knele we downe here in this presence,
                Besekyng that Lord of hy maugnefecens
215   That we ma see his hy exsellence,
                Yff thatt his swet wyll be.

3RD KING   Yondur, brothur, I see the star,
                Whereby I kno he ys nott far.
                Therefore, lordis, goo we nar
220   Into this pore place.

There the iij kyngis gois in to the jesen, to Mare and hir child.

1ST KING   Hayle, Lorde thatt all this worlde hathe wroght!
                Hale, God and man togedur in fere.
                For thow hast made all thyng of noght,
                Albeyt thatt thow lyist porely here;
225   A cupefull golde here I have the broght,
                In toconyng thow art without pere.

2ND KING   Hayle be thow, Lorde, of hy maugnyffecens!
                In toconyng of prestehod and dyngnete of offece,

---

199–201. Place your confidence in me, for there is nothing in my land which you cannot treat as if it were your own.

		To the I offur a cupefull off insence—
	230	For yt behovith the to have soche sacrefyce.

3RD KING

Hayle be thow, Lorde longe lokid fore.
I have broght the myre of mortalete,
In to-cunyng thow schalt mankynd restore
To lyff, be thy deyth apon a tre.

MARY   235

God have merce, kyngis, of yowre goodnes.
Be the gydyng of the Godhed hidder ar ye sent;
The provyssion off my swete sun your weyis whom
     reydres
And gostely reywarde you for youre present!
         The kings set out on their homeward journey.

IST KING

Syr kyngis, aftur owre promes,
240   Whome be Erode I must nedis goo.

2ND KING

Now truly, brethur, we can noo las;
But I am soo forwachid I wott not wat to do.

3RD KING

Right soo am I; wherefore I you pray,
Lett all us rest us awhyle upon this grownd.

IST KING   245

Brethur, your seying ys right well unto my pay.
The grace of thatt swet chylde save us all sownde!
     They lie down and, while they sleep, an angel appears.

ANGEL

Kyng of Tawrus, Sir Jespar,
Kyng of Arraby, Sir Balthasar,
Melchor, Kyng of Aginare,
250   To you now am I sent.
For drede of Eyrode, goo you west whom
Into those parties when ye cum downe.
Ye schal be byrrid with gret reynowne;
The Wholle Gost thus knoleyge hath sent.   *Exit.*

IST KING   255

Awake, sir kyngis, I you praye,
For the voise of an angell I hard in my dreyme.

---

231. Lord who has been long expected.
237–8. May the foresight of my sweet son direct your return journey and reward you in spiritual fashion for your gifts.
246. . . . keep us safe and sound.
251–2. Return west to those countries from which you came.

2ND KING		Thatt ys full tru thatt ye do sey, For he reyherssid owre names playne.

3RD KING		He bad thatt we schuld goo downe be west
	260	For drede of Eyrodis fawls betraye.
1ST KING		Soo for to do, yt ys the best.
		The child that we have soght, gyde us the wey!
		Now farewell, the feyrist of schapp soo swete!
		And thankid be Jesus of his sonde,
	265	Thatt we iij togeder soo suddenly schuld mete—
		Thatt dwell soo wyde and in straunge lond—
		And here make owre presentacion
		Unto this kyngis son, clensid soo cleyne,
		And to his moder, for oure salvacion;
	270	Of moche myrth no ma we meyne,
		Thatt we soo well hath done this obblacion.

2ND KING		Now farewell, Sir Jaspar, brothur, to yoeu—
		Kyng of Tawrus the most worthe;
		Sir Balthasar, also to you I bow;
	275	And I thanke you bothe of youre good cumpany
		Thatt we togeddur have had.
		He thatt made us to mete on hyll,
		I thanke hym now and eyver I wyll;
		For now may we goo withowt yll
	280	And of owre offerynge be full fayne.

3RD KING		Now syth thatt we must nedly goo,
		For drede of Erode thatt ys soo wrothe,
		Now farewell brothur, and brothur also,
		I take my leve here at you bothe
	285	This dey on fete.
		Now he thatt made us to mete on playne
		And offurde to Mare in hir jeseyne,
		He geve us grace in heyvin agayne
		All togeyder to mete! *Exeunt.*

---

260. In order to avoid false betrayal by Herod.

263. The sweetest and most beautiful of created things.

270–1. Now we can remember with great joy that we have performed this act of oblation.

285. *fete:* Craig's emendation. Sharp has *fote.*

Enter Herod and his attendants.

HERALD 290 Hayle, kynge most worthist in wede.

Hayle, manteinar of curtese throgh all this world wyde.

Hayle, the most myghtyst that eyver bestrod a stede.

Hayll, most monfullist mon in armor man to abyde.

Hayle, in thyne hoonowre.

295 Thesse iij kyngis that forthe were sent

And schuld have cum ageyne before the here present,

Another wey, lorde, whom the went,

Contrare to thyn honowre.

HEROD   Anothur wey! Owt! Owt! Owtt!

300 Hath those fawls trayturs done me this ded?

I stampe, I stare, I loke all abowtt.

Myght I them take, I schuld them bren at a glede.

I rent, I rawe, and now run I wode.

A! thatt these velen trayturs hath mard this my mode.

305 The schal be hangid, yf I ma cum them to!

Here Erode ragis in the pagond and in the strete also.

HEROD   E! and thatt kerne of Bedlem, he schal be ded

And thus schall I fordo his profece.

How sey you, Sir knyghtis, ys not this the best red,

Thatt all yong chyldur for this schuld be dede—

310 Wyth sworde to be slayne?

Then schall I, Erod, lyve in lede,

And all folke me dowt and drede,

---

293. The most manly man who waited in armour for his opponent.

296. And should have returned promptly here before you.

301. Herod's 'raging' is a guaranteed and expected dramatic highlight, a virtuoso display such as Chaucer's vain Absolon would have revelled in (the *Miller's Tale, C.T.* I. 3384). Cf. *Hamlet III.* iii.

302. If they were caught I should burn them at the stake.

304. A curse on these villains who have upset my reason.

305. . . . if I can get hold of them.

307. And in this way I shall controvert the prophecy about him.

		And offur to me bothe gold, rychesse, and mede,
		Thereto wyll the be full fayne.
IST KNIGHT	315	My lorde, kyng Erode be name,
		Thy wordis agenst my wyll schal be.
		To see soo many yong chylder dy ys schame,
		Therefore consell therto gettis thou non of me.
2ND KNIGHT		Well seyd, fello, my trawth I plyght.
	320	Sir kyng, perseyve right well you may,
		Soo grett a morder to see of yong frute
		Wyll make a rysyng in thi noone cuntrey.

HEROD   A rysyng! Owt, owt, owt.

There Erode ragis ageyne and then seyth thus:

		Owt, velen wrychis; 'har' apon you I cry.
	325	My wyll, utturly, loke that yt be wroght,
		Or apon a gallowse bothe you schall dy,
		Be Mahownde most myghtyste, that me dere hath boght.

IST KNIGHT   Now, cruell Erode, syth we schall do this dede—
                         Your wyll nedefully in this realme muste be wroght—
         330   All the chylder of that age dy the must nede.
                         Now with all my myght the schall be upsoght.

2ND KNIGHT   And I woll sweyre, here apon your bryght sworde:
                         All the chylder thatt I fynd, sclayne the schal be.
                         Thatt make many a moder to wepe
         335   And be full sore aferde
                         In owre armor bryght when the hus see.

HEROD   Now you have sworne, forth that ye goo,
                         And my wyll thatt ye wyrke bothe be dey and nyght;

---

314. They will be only too glad to do so (i.e. to offer him gifts).
320. You can see quite clearly.
322. Will occasion a revolt in your own land.
324. I cry 'harrow' against you. [Mod. colloquial—'have the law on you'.]
330. All the children of that age, they must be put to death.
336. When they see us (come) in our shining armour.

And then wyll I, for fayne, trypp lyke a doo.

340   But whan the be ded, I warne you, bryng ham
before my syght.

Exeunt Herod and attendants.

Joseph and Mary asleep—addressed by an angel.

ANGEL   Mare and Josoff, to you I sey—
Swete word from the fathur, I bryng you full ryght:
Owt of Bedlem into Eygype, forth goo ye the wey
And with you take the King, full of myght,

345   For drede of Eroddis rede.

JOSEPH   Aryse up Mare, hastely and sone;
Owre Lordis wyll nedys must be done,
Lyke ase the angell us bad.

MARY   Mekely, Josoff my none spowse,

350   Towarde that cuntrey let us reypeyre;
Att Eygyp sum tocun off howse,
God grant hus grace saff to cum there!

Here the wemen cum in wythe there chyldur, syngyng them; and Mare and Josoff goth awey cleyne.

1ST WOMAN   I lolle my chylde wondursly swete,
And in my narmis I do hyt kepe,

355   Becawse thatt yt schuld not crye.

2ND WOMAN   Thatt babe thatt ys borne in Bedlem so meke,
He save my chyld and me from velany!

3RD WOMAN   Be styll, be styll, my lyttull chylde.
That lorde of lordis save bothe the and me!

360   For Erode hath sworne with wordis wyld
Thatt all yong chyldur sclayne the schal be.

Enter the three knights.

1ST KNIGHT   Sey ye wyddurde wyvis, whydder ar ye awey?
What beyre you in youre armis nedis must we se.
Yff the be man chyldur, dy the must this dey,

365   For, at Eroddis wyll, all thyng must be.

---

339. For joy, I will dance like a doe.

351–2. God grant us grace to arrive safely in Egypt in some kind of house.
(There is no satisfactory solution for this line; Kittredge's emendation of the
line, 'Att Eygyp to sum cun off howse', is usually accepted.)

2ND KNIGHT And I in handis wonys them hent,
       Them for to sley noght woll I spare.
       We must fullfyll Erodis commandement—
       Elis be we asse trayturs and cast all in care.

1ST WOMAN 370 Sir knyghtis, of youre curtessee,
       Thys dey schame not youre chevaldre;
       But on my child have pytte
       For my sake in this styde.
       For a sympull sclaghtur yt were to sloo
    375 Or to wyrke soche a chyld woo—
       That can noder speyke nor goo,
       Nor never harme did.

2ND WOMAN He thatt sleyis my chyld in syght,
       Yff thatt my strokis on hym ma lyght,
    380 Be he skwyar or knyght,
       I hold hym but lost.
       Se, thow fawls losyngere,
       A stroke schalt thow beyre me here
       And spare for no cost.
     The women attack the knights as they snatch the children.

3RD WOMAN 385 Sytt he neyver soo hy in saddull,
       But I schall make his braynis addull;
       And here with my pott-ladull
       With hym woll I fyght.
       I shall ley on hym, as thogh I wode were,
    390 With thys same womanly geyre.
       There schall noo man steyre,
       Wheddur thatt he be kyng or knyght.
         The children are slain. The women lament.
1ST KNIGHT Who hard eyver soche a cry
       Of women thatt there chyldur have lost;
    395 And grettly reybukyng chewaldry

366–7. Once I have seized them with my hand, I will not spare to slay them.
371. Do not bring shame upon your oath of knighthood.
375–6. Or to injure such a child, that can neither walk nor talk.
391. No man shall dodge (my blows).

> Throgh-owt this reme in eyvere cost—
> Wyche many a mans lyff ys lyke to cost?
> For thys grett wreyche, that here ys done,
> I feyre moche wengance ther-off woll cum

2ND KNIGHT 400   E! brothur; soche talis may we not tell.
> Wher-fore, to the kyng lett us goo,
> For he ys lyke to beyre the perell,
> Wyche wasse the cawser that we did soo.
> Yett must the all be broght hym to
405   With waynis and waggyns fully fryght.
> I tro there wol be a carefull syght.   *Exeunt.*

The knights bring the children before Herod and his court.

IST KNIGHT   Loo! Eyrode, kyng, here mast thow see
> How many [thousand] thatt we have slayne.

2ND KNIGHT   And nedis thy wyll fullfullid must be;
410   There ma no mon sey there ageyne.

HERALD (*entering*)   Eyrode, kyng, I schall the tell—
> All thy dedis ys cum to noght;
> This chyld ys gone into Eygipte to dwell.
> Loo Sir, in thy none land what wondurs byn wroght!

HEROD 415   Into Eygipte! Alas for woo.
> Lengur in lande here I canot abyde.
> Saddull my palfrey, for in hast wyll I goo,
> Aftur yondur trayturs now wyll I ryde,
> Them for to sloo.
420   Now all men hy fast
> Into Eygipte in hast.
> All thatt cuntrey woll I tast,
> Tyll I ma cum them to.   *Exeunt.*

The end of the *Play of the Taylors and Scharmen.*
This matter was newly corrected by Robert Croo on 14th day of March, 1534.

---

396. In every corner of this kingdom.
400. That is no concern of ours.
404–5. For we have still to bring all of them to Herod in wains and waggons fully loaded.
410. No man may disobey his command.
414. Behold, Sire, what strange things have occurred in your own land.

D

Theise songes belonge to the Taylors and Shearemens Pagant. The first and the laste the shepheards singe and the second or middlemost the women singe.

SONG I

As I out rode this enderes night,
Of thre joli sheppardes I saw a sight,
And all a-bowte there fold a star shone bright;
  They sange terli terlow;
  So mereli the sheppards ther pipes can blow.

SONG II

Lully lulla thow littell tine child,
By by lully lullay thow littell tyne child,
  By by lully lullay!

O sisters too, how may we do
For to preserve this day
This pore yongling for whom we do singe
  By by lully lullay.

Herod the king in his raging,
Chargid he hath this day
His men of might in his owne sight
  All yonge children to slay,—

That wo is me pore child, for thee,
And ever morne and may
For thi parting neither say nor sing
  By by, lully lullay.

SONG III

Doune from heaven, from heaven so hie,
Of angeles ther came a great companie,
With mirthe and joy and great solemnitye,
  The sange terly terlow;
  So mereli the sheppards ther pipes can blow.

VII. The Woman Taken in Adultery

The Women Taken in Adultery is the 24th pageant in the *Ludus Coventriae;* it follows *The Temptation* (of Christ by Satan) and precedes *The Raising of Lazarus.* Probably the scribe believed that the play began with the Latin phrase '*Nolo mortem peccatoris*'—which precedes the first words of Jesus, as a kind of text before the pageant. There are blank pages in the manuscript both before and after this pageant. Stage directions are editorial.

MS: British Museum, Cotton Vespasian D.VIII

JESUS (*to the people*)   Man for thi synne take repentaunce:
                If thou amende that is amys,
                Than hevyn shal be thin herytaunce;
                Thow thou have don ayens God grevauns,
    5   Yett mercy to haske loke thou be holde;
                His mercy doth passe in trewe balauns
                All cruel jugement be many folde.

                Tho that your synnys be nevyr so grett
                For hem be sad and aske mercy;
    10   Sone, of my fadyr, grace ye may gett
                With the leste teer wepynge owte of your ey.
                My fadyr me sent the man to bye;
                All thi raunsom my-sylfe must pay;
                For love of the my-sylfe wyl dye—
    15   Iff thou aske mercy, I sey nevyr nay.

                In to the erth from hevyn a-bove—
                Thi sorwe to sese and joye to restore—
                Man, I cam down all for thi love.
                Love me ageyn; I aske no more.
    20   Thow thou mys-happe and synne ful sore
                Yit turne ayen and mercy crave;
                It is thi fawte and thou be lore—
                Haske thou mercy and thou shalt have.

4–8. Although you have grieved God (by sin), continue to seek for his mercy which, when all things are reckoned up, outweights many times over the severest judgement.

22. It is your own fault if you are lost (damned?).

Uppon thi neybore be not vengabyl,
25   Ageyn the lawe if he offende;
Lyke as he is, thou art unstabyl—
Thyn owyn frelte evyr thou attende.
Ever-more thi neybore helpe to amende
Evyn as thou woldyst he shulde the;
30   Ageyn hym wrath if thou accende
The same in happ wyll falle on the.

Eche man to othyr be mercyable
And mercy he shal have at nede;
What man of mercy is not tretable,
35   Whan he askyth mercy, he shal not spede.
Mercy to graunt, I com in dede;
Who so aske mercy, he shal have grace—
Lett no man dowte for his mysdede
But evyr aske mercy whyl he hath space.   *Exit.*

Enter a Scribe and a Pharisee.

SCRIBE   40   Alas, alas, oure lawe is lorn
A fals ypocryte, Jhesu be name—
That of a sheppherdis dowtyr was born—
Wyl breke oure lawe and make it lame.
He wyl us werke ryght mekyl shame,
45   His fals purpos if he up-holde;
All oure lawys he doth defame—
That stynkynge beggere is woundyr bolde.

PHARISEE   Sere scrybe, in feyth that ypocryte
Wyl turne this londe al to his lore;
50   Therfore I councell, hym to indyte
And chastyse hym ryght wel therfore.

26–7. Like him, you too are inclined to fall, so keep clearly in mind your own frailty.

30–31. If you burn with anger against him, probably it will recoil (later) on you.

39. While he has the opportunity.

43. And rob it of its power.

45. If he succeeds with his wicked plan.

SCRIBE

On hym be-leve many a score;
In his prechynge he is so gay
Ech man hym folwygh ever more and more;
55 Ayens that he seyth, no man seyth nay.

PHARISEE

A fals qwarel if we cowde feyne,
That ypocrite to puttyn in blame,
All his prechynge shulde sone disteyne
And than his wurchepp shuld turne to shame.
60 With sum falshede, to spyllyn his name,
Lett us assay his lore to spylle.
The pepyl with hym yff we cowde grame,
Than shulde we sone have al oure wyll.

INFORMER (entering) Herke, sere pharysew and sere scrybe,
65 A ryght good sporte I kan yow telle:
I undyr-take that ryght a good brybe
We all shul have to kepe councell.
A fayre yonge qwene here-by doth dwelle,
Both fresch and gay upon to loke,
70 And a tall man with here doth melle.
The wey in to hyre chawmere ryght evyn he toke.

Lett us thre, now, go streyte thedyr.
The wey full evyn I shall yow lede,
And we shul take them both to-gedyr
75 Whyll that thei do that synful dede.

SCRIBE

Art thou sekyr that we shal spede?
Shall we hym fynde whan we cum there?

INFORMER

Be my trowth, I have no drede
The hare fro the forme we shal a-rere.

56–7. If we could contrive a false debate in which we could put this hypocrite in the wrong.
62. If we could make the people angry with him.
66–7. I assure you we shall extort a handsome bribe in order to keep our mouths shut.
71. He has just made his way into her bedroom.
78–9. I am absolutely certain that we shall startle the hare in its lair.

PHARISEE   80   We shal have game and this be trewe;
                 Lete us thre werke by on assent.
                 We wyl here brynge evyn be-forn Jhesu
                 And, of here lyff, the truth present—
                 How in advowtrye hyre lyff is lent.
            85   Than hym be-forn whan she is browth,
                 We shul hym aske the trew judgement—
                 What lawfull deth to here is wrouth.

                 Of grace and mercy hevyr he doth preche,
                 And that no man shulde be vengeable;
            90   Ageyn the woman if he sey wrech,
                 Than of his prechynge he is unstable;
                 And, if we fynde hym varyable
                 Of his prechynge that he hath tawth,
                 Than have we cawse bothe juste and able
            95   For a fals man that he be cawth.

SCRIBE   Now, be grete God, ye sey ful well:
                 If we hym fyndyn in varyaunce,
                 We have good reson, as ye do tell,
                 Hym for to brynge to foule myschauns;
           100   If he holde stylle his dalyauns
                 And preche of mercy, hire for to save;
                 Than have we mater of gret substauns
                 Hym for to kylle and put in grave.

                 Grett reson why I shal yow telle—
           105   For Moyses doth bydde in oure lawe
                 That every advowterere we shuld qwelle
                 And yitt with stonyes thei shulde be slawe.
                 Ageyn Moyses if that he drawe
                 That synful woman with grace to helpe,
           110   He shal nevyr skape out of oure awe,
                 But he shal dye lyke a dogge whelpe.

---

90. If he asks for vengeance (i.e. the death penalty) against the woman.
95. We shall have good reason to arrest him as a false teacher.
108–9. If, contrary to the Law of Moses, he shows any tendency to show mercy to this sinful woman.

INFORMER		Ye tary ovyr-longe, serys, I sey yow;
		They wyl sone parte, as that I gesse.
		Therfore, if ye wyl have your pray now,
	115	Lete us go take them in here whantownnesse.

PHARISEE   Goo thou be-forn, the wey to dresse;
We shal the folwe with-in short whyle.
They move to another part of the stage.
If that we may that quene dystresse,
I hope we shal Jhesu be-gyle.

SCRIBE   120   Breke up the dore, and go we inne.
Sett to the shuldyr with all thi myght;
We shal hem take, evyn in here synne,
Here owyn trespas shal them indite.

A young man rushes out (of the house), in a state of undress, and carrying his breeches in his hand.

INFORMER   Stow that harlot, sum erthely wyght,
125   That in advowtrye here is fownde.

YOUTH   Yiff any man stow me this nyth,
I shal hym yeve a dedly wownde.
I, any man my wey doth stoppe,
Or we departe, ded shal I be;
130   I shal this daggare put in his croppe,
I shal hym kyll or he shal me.

PHARISEE   Grett Goddys curse mut go with the!
With suche a shrewe wyll I not melle.

YOUTH   That same blyssynge I yyff yow three
As he leaves the stage he speaks to the audience.
135   And qwheth yow alle to the devyl of helle.

In feyth, I was so sore affrayd
Of yone thre shrewys, the sothe to say;
My breche be nott yett well upteyd,
I had such hast to renne a-way.

---

116. You go in front and show us the way.

128-9. Ay! if any man stands in my way, one of us will die before we separate.

140 Thei shal nevyr cacche me in such affray.
 I am full glad that I am gon;
 Adewe, adewe a xx^{ti} devyl way
 And Goddys curse have ye everychon. *Exit.*

SCRIBE (*at the door*) Come forth thou stotte, com forth thou scowte,
 145 Com forth thou bysmare and brothel bolde;
 Com forth thou hore and stynkynge bych clowte.
 How longe hast thou such harlotry holde?

PHARISEE Com forth thou quene, com forth thou scolde,
 Com forth thou sloveyn, com forth thou slutte.
 150 We shal the tecche, with carys colde,
 A lytyl bettyr to kepe thi kutte.

WOMAN (*within*) A mercy, mercy, serys, I yow pray;
 For Goddys love, have mercy on me;
 Of my myslevyng me not be-wray.
 155 Have mercy on me, for charyte.

INFORMER Aske us no mercy; it shal not be.
 We shul so ordeyn for thi lott
 That thou shalt dye for thin advowtrye.
 Therefore com forth, thou stynkynge stott.

WOMAN 160 Serys, my wurchepp if ye wyl save
 And help I have non opyn shame,
 Bothe gold and sylvyr ye shul have,
 So that in clennes ye kepe my name.

SCRIBE Mede for to take, we were to blame;
 165 To save suche stottys, it shal not be.
 We shal brynge the to suche a game
 That all advowtererys shul lern be the.

150–1. We shall teach you, by means of sharp punishment, to know your proper place in the world.

154. Do not broadcast my evil way of life.

160–1. If, Sirs, you will protect my good name and ensure that I am not disgraced publicly.

166. We shall have such a game with you.

WOMAN   Stondynge ye wyl not graunt me grace,
                    But for my synne that I shal dye,
170   I pray yow, kylle me here in this place
                    And lete not the pepyl upon me crye.
                    If I be sclaundryd opynly,
                    To all my frendys it shul be shame:
                    I pray yow, kylle me prevyly—
175   Lete not the pepyl know my defame.

PHARISEE   Fy on the, scowte, the devyl the qwelle.
                    Ageyne the lawe shul we the kyll.
                    Fyrst shal hange the the devyl of helle,
                    Or we such folyes shulde fulfyll;
180   Thow it lyke the nevyr so ill,
                    Be-forn the prophete thou shalt have lawe.
                    Lyke as Moyses doth charge ut tyll,
                    With grett stonys thou shalt be slawe.

INFORMER   Com forth a-pase, thou stynkynge scowte.
185   Be-fore the prophete thou were this day,
                    Or I shal yeve the such a clowte
                    That thou shalt fall down evyn in the way.
                        He seizes the woman and leads her to Jesus.

SCRIBE   Now, be grett God, and I the pay,
                    Such a buffett I shal the take
190   That all the teth, I dare wel say,
                    Withinne thin heed for who shul shake.

PHARISEE   Herke, sere prophete; we all yow pray
                    To gyff trewe dom and just sentence
                    Upon this woman which, this same day,
195   In synfull advowtery hath don offense.

While they accuse the woman Jesus writes with his finger in the dust.

INFORMER   Se, we have brought here to your presens,

178–181. We would rather that the Devil in hell would hang you before we should consent to such foolishness—even though you will not like it, you shall be judged by Jesus.

182. Exactly as Moses ordains it. (Cf. *Leviticus* 20: 10).

190–1. Believe me, all the teeth in your head shall shake for misery.

196. See, we have brought her before you.

D*

Becawse ye ben a wyse prophete,
That ye shal telle, be consyens,
What deth to hyre ye thynke most mete.

SCRIBE   200   In Moyses lawe ryght thus we fynde,
That such fals lovers shul be slayn;
Streyte to a stake we shul hem bynde
And with grett stonys brest out ther brayn.
Of your concyens telle us the playn,
205   With this woman what shal be wrought.
Shall we lete here go qwyte agayn,
Or to hire deth shal she be brought?

Jesus does not reply but continues writing on the ground.

WOMAN   Now, holy prophete, be mercyable.
Upon me, wrecch, take no vengeaunce.
210   For my synnys abhomynable
In hert I have grett repentaunce.

I am wel wurthy to have myschaunce—
Both bodyly deth and werdly shame—
But, gracyous prophete, of socurraunce
215   This tyme pray yow, for Goddys name.

PHARISEE   Ageyn the lawe thou dedyst offens;
Therfore of grace speke thou no more.
As Moyses gevyth in law sentens.
Thou shalt be stonyd to deth therfore.

INFORMER   220   Ha don, sere prophete; telle us youre lore.
Shul we this woman with stonys kyll,
Or to hire hous hire home restore?
In this mater tell us your wyll.

SCRIBE   In a colde stodye me thynkyth ye sytt.
225   Good sere, awake; telle us your thought.
Shal she be stonyd? Telle us your wytt.
Or in what rewle shal scho be brought.

---

204. In your judgement of right and wrong tell us unequivocally.
206. Shall we release her without punishment.
214–15. Gracious prophet, in the name of God, I ask you to intercede for me this time.
227. What form of correction shall be imposed upon her?

JESUS   Loke, which of yow that nevyr synne wrought,
                   But is of lyff clennere than she,
230   Cast at here stonys and spare here nowght—
                   Clene out of synne, if that ye be.

Jesus once again stoops and writes on the ground and all the accusers leave in confusion by different exits.

PHARISEE   Alas, alas, I am ashamyd;
                   I am a-ferde that I shal deye.
                   All myn synnys, evyn propyrly namyd,
235   Yon prophyte dede wryte be-for myn eye.
                   Iff that my felawys that dude aspye,
                   They wyll telle it bothe fer and wyde:
                   My synfull levynge, if thei out crye,
                   I wot nevyr wher myn heed to hyde.

INFORMER   240 Alas, for sorwe myn herte doth blede:
                   All my synnes yon man dude wryte.
                   If that my felawys to them toke hede
                   I kan not me from deth acquyte.
                   I wolde I wore hyd sumwhere out of syght
245   That men shuld me nowhere se ne knowe.
                   Iff I be take, I am aflyght—
                   In mekyl shame I shal be throwe.

SCRIBE   Alas, the tyme that this be-tyd;
                   Ryght byttyr care doth me enbrace.
250   All my synnys be now unhyd—
                   Yon man, befor me, hem all doth trace.

                   If I were onys out of this place,
                   To suffyr deth gret and vengeauns able
                   I wyl nevyr come befor his face,
255   Thow I shuld dye in a stable.

---

236. If my companions saw all that.
243. I shall not be able to escape punishment by death.
245. That men could not see or recognize me.
252–5. If I could once get away from here—(as I must do), if I am to avoid a horrid death and the revenge that I am fit for—I should never appear before him, even though I were to die (as a beggar) in a stable.

WOMAN   Thow I be wurthy, for my trespas
                 To suffyr deth abhomynable,
                 Yitt, holy prophete, of your hygh grace
                 In your jugement be mercyable;
        260   I wyl nevyr more be so unstable.
                 O holy prophete, graunt me mercy
                 Of myn synnys unresonable—
                 With all myn hert I am sory.

JESUS   Where be thi fomen that dude the accuse?
        265   Why have thei left us to alone?
WOMAN   By-cawse they cowde nat hemself excuse,
                 With shame they fled hens everychone.
                 But, gracyous prophete, lyst to my mone—
                 Of my sorwe take compassyon,
        270   Now all myn enmyes hens be gone;
                 Sey me sum wurde of consolacion.

JESUS   For tho synnys that thou hast wrought
                 Hath any man condempnyd the?

WOMAN   Nay forsoth, that hath ther nought;
        275   But in your grace I putt me.

JESUS   For me thou shalt nat condempnyd be.
                 Go hom ageyn and walk at large;
                 Loke that thou leve in honeste
                 And wyl no more to synne, I the charge.

WOMAN   280   I thanke yow hyghly, holy prophete,
                 Of this grett grace ye have me graunt:
                 All my lewde lyff I shal doun lete
                 And fonde to be Goddys trewe servaunt.

DOCTOR   What man of synne be repentaunt,
        285   Of God if he wyl mercy crave,

280–1. Holy prophet, I thank you with all my heart for this great favour you have shown to me.

284. This final speech was first attributed to 'Jesus' and then the rubric was cancelled and 'Doctor' inserted. Presumably he was the commentator or expositor of the action.

285. If he will beg mercy from God.

God of mercy is so habundawnt
That what man haske it he shal it have.

Whan man is contrite and hath wonne grace,
God wele not kepe olde wreth in mynde,
290   But bettyr love to hem he has—
Very contryte whan he them fynde.
Now God, that dyed for all mankende,
Save all these pepyl, both nyght and day,
And of oure synnys he us unbynde
295   Hyghe lorde of hevyn that best may.

                                        Amen.

294-5. And may he, supreme lord of heaven, who is best able to, release us from our sins.

VIII. The Conspiracy

The Conspiracy (and *Capture of Christ*), the twentieth pageant in the Towneley Cycle, is the longest of the thirty-two extant plays. The following extract forms the first half of the play; the remainder follows the Gospel narrative of the Last Supper, the visit to Olivet, the scene in Gethsemane, the betrayal of Christ by Judas and His appearance before Caiaphas. The text, composed around 1450, is in the North-eastern Midland dialect; stage directions are editorial.
MS: Huntingdon HM1.

PILATE
        Peas, carles, I commaunde, unconand I call you;
        I say stynt and stande, or foull myght befall you.
        Fro this burnyshyd brande, now when I behald you,
        I red ye be shunand, or els the dwill skald you,
5   At onys.
        I am kyd, as men knawes,
        Leyf leder of lawes;
        Seniours, seke to my sawes,
        For bryssyng of youre bonys.

10   Ye wote not wel, I weyn, what wat is commen to
           the towne,
        So comly cled and cleyn, a rewler of great renowne;
        In sight, if I were seyn, the granser of great
           Mahowne;
        My name Pylate has beyn; was never kyng with
           crowne
        More worthy;
15   My wysdom and my wytt,
        In sete here as I sytt,
        Was never more lyke it,
        My dedys thus to dyscry.

6–7. As everyone knows, I am famous as the dear prince of laws.

9. To prevent bruising (by punishment) of your bones.

10–11. You have not been told what kind of man has come to this town, so beautifully dressed. . . .

15–18. As I sit here on my throne, if my famous deeds were described to you, no one could compare with me for wisdom and intelligence.

For I am he that may make or mar a man;
20 Myself if I it say, as men of cowrte now can,
Supporte a man to day, to-morn agans hym than,
On both parties thus I play, and fenys me to ordan
The right;
Bot all fals indytars,
25 Quest-mangers and jurers,
And all thise fals out-rydars,
Ar welcom to my sight.

More nede had I never of sich servand now, I say
        you;
So can I well consider the trowth, I most displeas
        you,
30 And therfor com I hedyr; of peas, therfor, I pray
        you.
Ther is a lurdan ledyr I wold not shuld dysmay you
A-bowtt;
A prophete is he prasyd,
And great unright has rasyd;
35 Bot, be my banys her blasid,
His deth is dight no dowtt.

He prechys the pepyll here—that fature fals
        Jhesus—
That, if he lyf a yere, dystroy oure law must us;
And yit I stand in fere; so wyde he wyrkys vertus,
40 No fawt can on hym bere no lyfand leyde tyll us.
Bot sleyghtys
Agans hym shall be soght,
That all this wo has wroght;
Bot on his bonys it shall be boght—
45 So shall I venge oure rightys.

20–1. As judges now do in court, if I speak the word I can support a man today and down him tomorrow.

22–3. . . . and pretend to carry out justice.

31–2. There is an evil waster about whom I do not really wish to talk to you.

38. If he lives one (more) year, we will have to abandon our law.

40. No one alive can bring to us any (tale of a) fault in him.

44. He shall pay for it with his body.

That fatoure says, that thre shuld ever dwell in oone
    godhede,
That ever was and shall be sothfast in man-hede.
He says, of a madyn born was he, that never toke
    mans sede.
And that his self shall dy on tre—and mans sawll out
    of preson lede.

50   Let hym alone—
    If this be true in deyd—
    His spech shall spryng and sprede,
    And over-come ever ylkone.

CAIAPHAS   Syr pilate, prynce of mekyll price,
55   That prevyd is withoutten pere,
    And lordyngys that oure laws in lyse,
    On oure law now must us lere
    And of oure warkys we must be wyse,
    Or els is all oure welthe in were.
60   Therfor say sadly youre avyse,
    Of hedus harmes that we have here—
    Towchyng that tratoure strang—
    That makys this beleyf.
    For if he may thus furth gang,
65   It will over greatly grefe.

ANNAS   Sir, oure folk ar so afrayd—
    Thrugh lesyns he losys oure lay—

---

47. Actually in one human nature.

50–3. If this be really true and we leave him alone, his doctrine will flourish and take the place of all other teaching.

54. Pilate's speech was in the nine-line stanza form normally used by the 'Wakefield Master'; the rest of the play follows the regular pattern, *ababababcdcd*, which, like so many of the metres in this cycle, is derived from the favourite metres employed in fourteenth-century England. The pattern of events in this play is a conflation of all four Gospel narratives. See *Matthew* 26: 3–5, 14–16; *Mark* 11: 27–9, 12: 13–7; *Luke* 22: 2–6; *John* 18: 28–38.

56. And you lords, the guardians of our law.

57. We must now learn from our law.

64–5. For if he is allowed to go ahead, considerable damage will result.

67. Because of the lies he imputes to our law.

		Som remedy must be rayd
		So that he weynd not thus away.
PILATE	70	Now certan, syrs, this was well sayd,
		And I assent right as ye say—
		Som prevay poynt to be purvayd
		To mar his myght if we may.
		And therfor, sirs, in this present,
	75	What poynt so were to prase,
		Let all be at assent;
		Let se what ilk man says.
CAIAPHAS		Sir, I have sayde you here beforne
		His soteltyes and grefys so sare;
	80	He turnes oure folk, bothe even and morne,
		And ay makys mastres mare and mare.
ANNAS		Sir, if he skape, it were great skorne;
		To spyll hym tytt, we will not spare.
		For, if oure lawes were thusgatys lorne,
	85	Men wold say it were lake of lare.
PILATE		For certan, syrs, ye say right weyll
		For to wyrk witterly.
		Bot yit som fawt must we feyll,
		Wherfor that he shuld dy;
	90	And therfor, sirs, let se youre saw—
		For what thyng we shuld hym slo.
CAIAPHAS		Sir, I can rekyn you on a raw
		A thowsand wonders—and well moo—
		Of crokyd men (that we well knaw)—
	95	How graythly that he gars them go;
		And ever he legys agans oure law,
		Tempys oure folk and turnys us fro.

72–3. In secret if it can be done—we must find some treacherous point of law by means of which we can diminish his power.

78–9. I have already recounted his sophistries and bitter attacks.

81. And continually encourages revolt against authority.

84. If our laws should lose their authority in this way.

88. We must clearly find some error (of his) for which he must die.

95–7. How easily he makes them (i.e. the crippled) walk and all the time he attacks our law, tempting our people and turning them against us.

ANNAS		Lord, dom and defe, in oure present
		Delyvers he, by downe and dayll;
	100	What hurtys or harmes thay hent,
		Full hastely he makys theym hayll.
		And for sich warkys, as he is went,
		Of ilk welth he may avayll;
		And unto us he takys no tent,
	105	Bot ilk man trowes unto his tayll.
PILATE		Yei, dewill! And dos he thus—
		As ye well bere wytnes?
		Sich fawte fall to us,
		Be oure dom, for to redres.

CAIAPHAS	110	And also, sir, I have hard say
		An other noy, that neghys us nere:
		He will not kepe oure sabate day—
		That holy shuld be haldyn here—
		Bot forbedys far and nere
	115	To wyrk at oure bydyng.
PILATE		Now, by Mahowns bloode so dere,
		He shall aby this bowrdyng!
		What dewill will he be there?
		This hold I great hethyng.
ANNAS	120	Nay, nay, well more is ther.
		He callys hym self 'hevens kyng'
		And says that he is so myghty
		All rightwytnes to rewll and red.
PILATE		By Mahowns blood, that shall he aby
	125	With bytter baylls, or I ett bred.

---

99. By down and dell—a tag for 'all over the place'.

102–103. And because of such deeds—which he is supposed (to perform)—he can get whatever money he pleases.

105. But every man believes in his gospel.

108–9. According to our (Roman) law, it is our task to punish this (particular) crime (i.e. levying a personal tribute).

111. A second offence that affects us (Jews) closely.

115. To do as we command.

117–18. He shall pay for this joke! In the devil's name, what does he mean by this one?

1ST KNIGHT		Lord, the loth Lazare of Betany—
		That lay stynkand in a sted—
		Up he rasyd bodely
		The fourt day after he was ded.
2ND KNIGHT	130	And for that he hym rasyd,
		That had lyne ded so long a space,
		The people hym full mekyll prasyd
		Over all, in every place.
ANNAS		Emangys the folke has he the name
	135	That he is Godys son, and none els;
		And his self says the same—
		That his fader in heven dwelles;
		That he shall rewll both wyld and tame.
		Of all sich maters thus he mels.
PILATE	140	This is the dwylls payn.
		Who trowys sich talys as he tels?
CAIAPHAS		Yis, lord, have here my hand;
		And ilk man beyldys hym as his brother.
		Sich whaynt cantelys he can,
	145	Lord, ye knew never sich an othere.
PILATE		Why, and wotys he not that I have
		Bold men to be his bayn?
		I commaunde both knyght and knave—
		Sesse not to that lad be slayn.
1ST KNIGHT	150	Sir Pylate, mefe you now no more,
		Bot mese youre hart and mend youre mode.
		For bot if that losell lere oure lore
		And leyf his gawdys, he were as good.
		For in oure tempyll we will not spare
	155	To take that losell, if he were woode.

138–9. That he shall rule everything on earth. He prates a great deal about these particular topics.

142. Indeed they do, my lord; I am ready to take my oath on it.

144. He knows so many clever tricks (practices).

146–7. I have valiant soldiers who can put him to death.

149. Do not give up until this fellow is dead.

150–1. Do not disturb yourself further—soothe your heart and calm your anger.

152–3. Unless that vagabond follows our advice and abandons his tricks, he's as good as dead.

PILATE		In oure tempyll? The dwill! What dyd he thare?
		That shall he by, by Mahouns blode!
2ND KNIGHT		Lord, we wist not youre wyll.
		With wrang ye us wyte.
	160	Had ye so told us tyll,
		We shuld have takyn hym tyte.

PILATE		The dwill, he hang you high to dry!
		Whi, wold ye lese oure lay?
		Go, bryng hym heder hastely,
	165	So that he weynd not thus away.
CAIAPHAS		Sir Pilate, be not to hasty,
		Bot suffer over oure sabote day.
		In the mene tyme—to spyr and spy
		Mo of his mervels, if men may.
ANNAS	170	Yei, sir, and when this feste is went,
		Then shall his craftys be kyd.
PILATE		Certys, syrs, and I assent
		For to abyde then, as ye byd.

Judas enters.

JUDAS		Masters, myrth be you emang,
	175	And mensk be to this meneye.
CAIAPHAS		Go! Othere gatys thou has to gang
		With sorow. Who send after the?
JUDAS		Syrs, if I have done any wrang,
		At youre awne bydyng will I be.
PILATE	180	Go hence, harlot! Hy mot thou hang!
		Where in the dwill hand had we the?

---

163. Would you ignore our law?
167. But wait until after our Sabbath day.
174. For a thorough examination of the medieval legends developed around the story of Judas see P. F. Baum, 'The Medieval Legend of Judas Iscariot', *P.M.L.A.*, xxxi (1916), 481–632.
175. All honour to this company.
179. I shall do just as you command.
181. Who the devil found you for us?

JUDAS		Goode sir, take it to no grefe.
		For my menyng it may avayll.
ANNAS		We, lad, thou shuld ask lefe
	185	To com in sich counsayll.

JUDAS		Sir, all youre counsell well I ken;
		Ye mene my master for to take.
ANNAS		A ha! here is oone of his men
		That thus unwynly gars us wake.
PILATE	190	La hand on hym, and hurl hym then
		Emangys you, for his master sake;
		For we have maters, mo then ten,
		That well more myster were to make.
CAIAPHAS		Set on hym buffettys sad—
	195	Sen he sich mastrys mase—
		And teche ye sich a lad
		To profer hym in sich a place.

JUDAS		Sir, my profer may both pleas and pay
		To all the lordys in this present.
PILATE	200	We! go hens in xx dwill way!
		We have no tome, the for to tent.
JUDAS		Yis, the profete—that has lost youre lay
		By wonder warkys, as he is went—
		If ye will sheynd hym, as ye say—
	205	To sell hym you, I wyll assent.
PILATE		A, sir, hark! What says thou?
		Let se, and shew thi skyll.

---

183. What I intend to say will explain everything.

184–5. Eh! lad, you should ask permission before you break into such a secret meeting.

189. Who, in this unfriendly way, gives us a jolt.

192–3. We have more than enough things to decide which cry out for our attention.

195. Since he acts above his station.

197. To offer advice (to us) here.

202–3. Who has undermined your religion by his miracles—as he is supposed (to perform).

207. Be clear and explain your reason (argument).

JUDAS		Sir, a bargan bede I you.
		By it, if ye will.
ANNAS	210	What is thi name? Do tell in hy—
		If we may wit, if thou do wrang.
JUDAS		Judas Scarioth, so hight I,
		That with the profet has dwellyd lang.

PILATE		Sir, thou art welcom witterly!
	215	Say what thou will us here emang.
JUDAS		Not els, bot if ye will hym by.
		Do say me sadly, or I gang.
CAIAPHAS		Yis, freynd, in fathe will we,
		Noght els. Bot hartely say
	220	How that bargan may be –
		And we shall make the pay.

ANNAS		Judas, for to hold the hayll
		And for to fell all fowll defame,
		Looke that thou may avow thi sayll;
	225	Then may thou be withoutten blame.
JUDAS		Sir, of my teyn gyf ye never tayll,
		So that ye have hym here at hame.
		His bowrdyng has me broght in bayll,
		And, certys, his self shall have the same.
CAIAPHAS	230	Sir Pylate, tentys here tyll
		And lightly leyf it noght;
		Then may ye do youre wyll
		Of hym that ye have boght.

ANNAS		Yei, and then may we be bold,
	235	Fro all the folk to hald hym fre;
		And hald hym hard with us in hold,
		Right as oone of youre meneye.

---

216. Not a word unless you will pay for him.
221. And we shall give you every satisfaction.
224. See to it that you give oaths which bind your own soul.
226. Don't bother your head about my damnation.
230–1. Probe into this and do not believe it lightly.
234–7. And then, boldly, we can keep him away from all the people, and hide him closely in our stronghold as though he were one of your followers.

PILATE   Now, Judas, sen he shal be sold,
                    How lowfes thou hym? Belyfe, let se.

JUDAS   240   For xxx pennys truly told,
                    Or els may not that bargan be.
                    So mych gart he me lose,
                    Malycyusly and yll;
                    Therfor ye shall have chose—
     245   To by, or let be styll.

ANNAS   Gart he the lose? I pray the, why?
                    Tell us now pertly, or thou pas.

JUDAS   I shall you say, and that in hy,
                    Every word, right as it was.

     250   In Symon house, with hym sat I
                    With othere meneye that he has;
                    A woman cam to company,
                    Callyng hym 'lord'; sayng, 'alas!'
                    For synnes that she had wroght,
     255   She wepyd sore always;
                    And an oyntment she broght—
                    That precyus was to prayse.

                    She weshyd hym with hir terys weytt,
                    And sen dryed hym with hir hare;
     260   This fare oyntment—hir bale to beytt—
                    Apon his hede she put it thare,
                    That it ran all abowte his feytt.
                    I thoght it was a ferly fare.
                    The house was full of odowre sweytt;
     265   Then, to speke, myght I not spare—
                    For, certys, I had not seyn
                    None oyntment half so fyne—

---

239. What's your value on him? Quickly, show us.
242. This is the exact amount of the loss he caused to me.
245. To buy—or leave things as they are.
246-7. Caused you to lose? Why, I ask you? Tell us in detail, before you go.
250. Cf. *Mark* 14: 3-11.
260. —in order to compensate for her misfortune—
263. I thought it very odd behaviour indeed.
265. I could not restrain myself from making a comment.

Ther-at my hart had teyn,
Sich tresoure for to tyne.

270   I sayd it was worthy to sell
Thre hundreth pens in oure present,
For to parte poore men emell.
Bot will ye se wherby I ment:
The tent parte, truly to tell,

275   To take to me was myne intent—
For, of the tresure that to us fell,
The tent parte ever with me went.
And if iii hundreth be right told,
The tent parte is even thryrty.

280   Right so he shal be sold;
Say, if ye will hym by.

PILATE   Now for certan, sir, thou says right wele—
Sen he wate the with sich a wrast—
For to shape hym som uncele

285   And for his bost be not abast.

ANNAS   Sir, all thyn askyng, every dele
Here shall thou hafe; therof be trast.
Bot looke that we no falshede fele.

JUDAS   Sir, with a profe may ye frast:

290   All that I have here hight
I shall fulfill in dede,
And well more at my myght,
In tyme when I se nede.

PILATE   Judas, this spekyng must be spar,

295   And neven it never, nyght ne day.
Let no man wyt where that we war,
For ferdnes of a fowll enfray.

269–71. (To see) such costly (ointment) being wasted. I said that it would fetch 300 pence today, which could be shared among the poor.

273. But if you wish to know what my real purpose was.

279–80. The tenth of that is exactly 30 and for this precise amount he shall be sold.

283–4. Since he has hurt you by this trick—you are right to plan some injury against him.

289. You may test and prove me.

292. And much more to the best of my ability.

296–7. Let no one know what we have planned, in case we have a wild riot.

CAIAPHAS		Sir, therof let us moyte no mare.
		We hold us payde; take ther thi pay.
		Giving the money to Judas.
JUDAS	300	This gart he me lose lang are;
		Now ar we even, for onys and ay.
ANNAS		This forwarde will not fayll—
		Therof we may be glad.
		Now were the best counsayll,
	305	In hast that we hym had.
PILATE		We shall hym have, and that in hy,
		Full hastely here in this hall.
		Sir knyghtys, that ar of dede dughty,
		Stynt never in stede ne stall,
	310	Bot looke ye bryng hym hastely—
		That fatur fals—what so befall.
IST KNIGHT		Sir, be not abast therby,
		For, as ye byd, wyrk we shall. *Exeunt.*

300-1. This is the amount he made me lose before; now we are quits once and for all.

309. Do not delay for an instant.

312-13. Have no fears on that score. We shall do exactly as you command.

IX. Christ's Passion

Christ's Passion is the sixteenth pageant in the *Chester Plays* and was presented by *The Bowers, Fletchers and Ironmongers.* The following selection forms the second half of the pageant after the procession has arrived at Calvary for the Crucifixion. At the end of the pageant, the scribe has written the date 27 July 1607. The stage directions in the following text are editorial in origin. *Dialect:* (Late) North-western Midland.
MS: British Museum, Harleian 2124.

Jesus and the two thieves are led away and the women followers of Jesus enter.

1ST WOMAN		Alas, alas, and woe is me.
		A dolefull sight is it to se:
		So many saved hath he,
		And now goes his way!
2ND WOMAN	5	Sorowfull may his mother be
		To witt the flesh—so fayr and free—
		Nayled so fowle upon a tree,
		As he must be today.
JESUS		Yee women of Jerusalem,
	10	Weeps not for me, nor makes no swem;
		But for your own barnteame
		You may wepe tenderlye.
		For tyme shall come, without weer,
		They shall blesse belye that never child beare,
	15	And papps that never milk came neare—
		So much is your anoy.

Jesus ascends the hill of Calvary.

CAIAPHAS		Have done, ye tormentors, tyte!
		Spoyl him that hath done us spyte.
1ST JEW		Yea, though he both pisse and shyte,
	20	Out he shal be shaken.
		Be thou wroth, be thou fayne,

---

6. To know that such a beautiful and noble body will be nailed . . .
14. They will bless the barren womb.
16. So bitter will your suffering be.

I will be thy chamberlayne.
This coat getts thou never agayne,
And I be waken.

2ND JEW 25 This coat shall be myne
For it is good and fyne,
And seam is ther none within—
That I can see.

3RD JEW   Yea, God geve me pyne,
30 And that shal be thyne.
Aye thou art enclyne
To draw toward thee.

4TH JEW   Nay, fellow, by my fay,
At the dyce we will play,
35 And ther we shall assay
This weed for to wynne.

1ST JEW   Yea, fellow, by my fay
Well canst thou say.
Lay forth thes cloths; lay
40 On board, or we blinne!

They strip the clothes from Jesus who stands naked while they play dice.

2ND JEW   Fellow, now letts se—
Here are dyce three—
Which of all we
Shall wynne this ware.

3RD JEW 45 Nay, departed it shal be—
For that is equitye—
In fowr parts, as mott I thee,
Or we heathen fare.

4TH JEW   This coat without seame,
50 To break it were sweme;

---

24. As long as I'm aware of it.
31-2. You always tend to do things to your own advantage.
33. Cf. *Matthew* 27: 33-8.
39-40. Lay out the clothes. Bring out the board (for dicing) straight away.
43-4. Which of us three will win this stuff.
48. Before we leave here.

| | For in Jerusalem |
| | Ther is none suche, verament. |

1ST JEW   His dame now may dream
For her barnteam,
55   For neither aunt nor eame
Getts this garment.

2ND JEW   His other clothes all
To us fowr mon fall;
First depart them I shall—
60   And after dice for this. *Holds up the seamless robe.*
This kirtell myne I call,
And take thou this pall;
         Dividing the various garments among them.
Each man in this hall
Wotts I do not amisse.

65   This corsett take to thee,
And thou this to thy fee.
Eche man may see
That all we be served.

3RD JEW   Yea, I redd now that we
70   Sytt down, so mott I thee.
And loke whos this shall be
That is here reserved.   *They sit down to play.*

1ST JEW   Now will I beginne
To cast, or I blynne,
75   This coate for to wynne—
That is good and fyne.   *He throws and loses.*

2ND JEW   By my father kynne,
No part hast thou in.
But, or I heathen twynne,
80   This coat shall be myne.
Take here, I darr lay
A rowndfull, in good fay.   *Throws and loses.*

---

78. You've lost your share in it.
79. Before I leave this place.
81–2. Watch this. I bet I'll throw a 'roundfull' (cf. 'Full house'?).

3RD JEW   Thou fayles, by my fay,
               To have this to thy fee.
        85   For it was cater trey,
               Therfor goe thou thy way—
               And as well thou may—
               And leave it with me.   *Throws and loses.*

4TH JEW   Fellows, verament,
        90   I redd you all assent,
               This gay garment,
               That is without seame,
               You geve (by my judgment)
He speaks in short phrases as he throws and wins by throwing a 'six'.
               To me; this vestament.
        95   For syyes God has sent,
               Think ye never so swem.

1ST JEW   As have I good grace,
               Wonne it thou hase;
               For syyes ther was—
       100   Each man might see.
                                  Shows winning dice to the audience.

CAIAPHAS   Men, for cockes face,
               How longe shall Poydrace
               Stand naked in this place.
               Goe, neyles him to the tree.

2ND JEW   105 Anon, maister, anon.
               A hammer have I one—
               As farr as I have gone,
               Ther is not such another.
3RD JEW   And here are, by my bones,
       110   Neiles, very good ones,
               To neyle therupon—
               Though he weare my brother.

---

85. It was a 'four' and a 'three' (French terms).
95–6. Since God has given me a 'six', don't curse your bad luck.
97. As I hope to be saved.
102. *Poydrace*—term of abuse for Jesus. (? Dirty-arse).
106–8. Wherever I've travelled I've never found a hammer like this one of mine.

4TH JEW		Goe we to hit fast.
		This caytyfe I have cast,
	115	Shall be wronge wrast,
		Or I wend away.
1ST JEW		Here is a rope will last
		For to draw a maste.
		This poplard never past
	120	So perilous a play.

2ND JEW   Lay him therupon,   *They lay Jesus on the cross.*
     This ilke mased mon,
     And I shall dryve on
     This neile to the ende.

3RD JEW   125   As broke I my pan,
     Well cast him I can;
     He shall be well wonne,
     Or I from him wend.

4TH JEW   Fellows, will ye see
   130   How sleight I will be,
     This fyst or I flye,
     Here to make fast.

1ST JEW   Yea, but as mott I thee,
     Short-armed is he—
   135   To bringe to this tree
     It will not long last.

2ND JEW   Ha, therfore care thou nought—
     A sleight I have sought:
     Ropes must be brought,
   140   To strean him with strength.

3RD JEW   A rope, as behight,
     You shall have, unbought.

115–16. Will be severely and firmly twisted before I go.
117–18. A rope strong enough to hoist a mast.
126. I know how to fix him.
131–2. To make this fist secure before I've done.
135–6. His arms are not long enough to reach across the tree.
138. I know a dodge for that one.
140. To stretch him out by pulling on the ropes.
141–2. Almost—'One well-made rope coming up! Nothing to pay!'

> Take here one, well-wrought,
> And draw him on length.

They tie a rope to the left hand while the right is being secured (with a nail).

4TH JEW	145	Draws, for your father kynne!
		Whyle that I dryve in
		This ilke iron pinne—
		That, I dare lay, will last.
1ST JEW		As ever have I wynne,
	150	His arme is but a fynne.
		Now dryves on, but dinne,
		And we shall draw fast.

2ND JEW   Fellows, by this light,
           Three of them pull and the fourth fixes the nail.
    Now if his feet were pight,
155   This gommon went aright,
    And up he should be raysed.

3RD JEW   That shall be done in height—
    Anone in your sight.
    For my trothe I plight,
160   I deserve to be praysed.   *They transfix the feet.*

4TH JEW (*to the audience*)   Fellows, will ye see,
    How I have stretcht his knee?
    Why prayse you not me
    That have so well done?

1ST JEW   165   Yea, help now that hee
    On height raysed be;
    For, as mott I thee,
    Almost it is none.

Pilate, with a scroll in his hand, gives orders to a soldier.

PILATE   Come hither, thou. I commande thee.
   170   Goe, neile this table on the tree.
    Sith he Kinge of Jews will be,
    He must have cognisaunce.

---

149. As I hope for joy in Heaven.
151–2. Now strike—and clang!—while we pull hard.
155. This chap would be placed properly.

'Jesu of Nazareth' men may see,
'Kinge of Jews', how lykes ye?
175 I writt theron, for so sayd he,
Without variaunce.

2ND JEW

Now, Sir Pilat, to us take hede:
Kinge he is not, as God me spede.
Therfore thou doest a sory deed—
180 That writinge many one rews.
Thou should wryte that many might reade,
How he lyed to eche leede,
And towld, overall wher he yeede,
That he was Kinge of Jewes.

PILATE   185 That is written, that have I written.
3RD JEW   Yea, would God thou were beshitten.
For all men shall well witten
That wrong thou hast wrought.
What the Devill. Kinge is he none,
190 But falcsly, ther as he hath gone,
Towld leasings to many one—
That full dear shal be bought.

They all raise up the cross and Mary, the mother of Christ, enters with three other women.

MARY

Alas, my love, my lyfe, my lee,
Alas. Mowrning now madds me.
195 Alas, my boote looke thou be,
Thy mother that thee bare!
Thinke on my freut. I fosterd thee,
And gave the sucke upon my knee;

175–6. I have written down unaltered the title he himself claimed.
180. That piece of writing will be regretted by many.
183. And claimed, everywhere he went. . . .
185. Cf. *John* 19: 22.
192. (Those lies) will be paid for dearly.
193. Based on *John* 19: 25–7 and *Mark* 15: 40–1.
195–7. Alas! May you be the salvation of me, the mother that bore you. Think on (me) my offspring.

Upon my payne have thou pitty.
200   Thee faylës no power.

Alas, why ne were my lyfe forlorne?
To fynd my foodë, me beforne
Tugged, lugged, all totorne
With traytors, now this tyde;
205   With neilës, thrust, and crown of thorne.
Therfore I madd, both even and morne,
To see my birth, that I have borne,
This bitter bale to byde.

My sorrow, sweet sonne, thou cease,
210   Or, of my lyfe, thou me releace.
How should I apayd be, or in peace,
To se thee in such penaunce?
Sith thou me to thy moder chose
And of my body borne thou was,
215   As I conceived thee wemlesse,
Thou graunt me some legiaunce.

Alas. The sorrow of this sight
Marrs my mynd, mayne, and might;
But aye my hart me think is light
220   To looke on that I love.
And when I look anon right
Upon my child, that thus is dight,
Would death deliver me in height,
Then were I all above.

225   Alas, my sorrow, why wilt thou not slake,
And to thes traytours me betake,
To suffer death, sonne, for thy sake,
And doe as I thee say?

---

200. You can do anything.
208. Having to suffer this grievous torment.
213–14. Since you chose me as your mother and were born of my body.
223–4. If death would deliver me quickly, I should be placed above ('all suffering' or 'all other people').

Alas, theefes, why doe ye so?
230 Slay me, and let my sonne goe.
For him, suffer I would this woe
And lett him wend his way.

MARY MAGDALENE   Alas, how should my hart be light,
To see my semely lord, in sight
235 Dilfully drawn and all todigt,
That did nevar man grevance.
Marred I am, mayne and might,
And for him me fayles to feight;
But God, that aye rules the right,
240 He geve you much mischance!

MARY, MOTHER OF JAMES   Alas, sorrow settes me sore—
Mirth of thee gett I no more.
Why wouldst thou dye, Jesus, wherfore?
That to the dead gave lyfe.

245 Help me, Jesu, with some thinge,
And out of this bitter bale me bringe;
Or ells slay me, for any thinge,
And stint me of this stryfe.

Come, lord, downe, and breake thy bandes.
250 Loce and heale thy lovely handes.
Or tell, Jesu, for whom thy woundes,
Since thou art God and man.

MARY SALOME   Alas, that ever I borne was,
To se my lord in such unpeace;
255 My sorrow will never slake ne cease—
Such sorrow is me upon.

ANNAS   Now this shrew is hoven an height,
I would se, for all his sleight,

---

234. To see my virtuous lord, before my eyes.
238. And I am unable to fight for him.
240. May he bring misfortune upon you.
245. With some kind of reasoned comfort.
247-8. Or else slay me, in spite of every thing (i.e. let nothing stop you), and so put an end to my complaint.
251-2. Or else, Jesus, since you are God and Man, explain why you are wounded.

    For his croune how he would feight,
260 And fownd from us to flee.
    He that hath healed so many one,
    Now save him selfe—if that he can—
    And we shall leeve him upon
    That Gods sonne is he.

Jesus, hanging in bonds, cries out:
JESUS   265 Father, if thy will be,
    Forgeve them this they done to me.
    They be blynd, and may not see
    How fowle the do amisse.

CAIAPHAS   If thou be of such posty,
270 And Gods sonne in majesty,
    Come downe, and we will leeve on thee
    That soothly so it is.

1ST THIEF   If thou be Christ veray
    And Gods sonne; now assay—
275 Save us from this death today,
    And thy selfe also.

2ND THIEF *(to his companion)* Ah, man; be still, I thee pray—
    Dred God, so I reed thee aye—
    For folishly thou speaks, in fay;
280 Make not thy frend thy foe.

    Man, thou knows well, iwysse,
    That righteously we suffer this;
    But this man hath not done amis,
    To suffer so great anoye.
(To Jesus) 285 But, lord, I beseech thee,
    When thou art in thy majesty,
    Then that thou wilt thinke on me
    And on me have mercy.

259–60. How he would fight for his crown and try to escape from us.
261. Cf. *Matthew* 27: 42.
266. Cf. *Luke* 23: 34.
271–2. And we will believe that you truly are God's son.
273. Cf. *Luke* 23: 39.
278. Fear God, as I advise you to do at all times.

JESUS		Man, I tell thee in good fay,
	290	For thy beleefe is so veray,
		In Paradice thou shalt be today
		With me in my blisse.
		And to thee, woman also, I say:
		Ther thy sonne thou se may,
	295	That clean virgin hase bene aye—
		Lyke as thy self is.
		And, John, thy moder ther may thou se.
JOHN EVANGELIST		Yea, lord, her keper I will be.
		Welcome Mary, mother free,
	300	Togeather we must goe.
MARY		Alas, my hart will break in three.
		Alas, death, I conjure thee.
		My lyfe, sonne, thou take from me
		And twin me from this woe.
JOHN EVANGELIST		Comfort thee, swet Mary.
		Though we suffer this anye,
		I tell the, suster, sickerly,
		On lyfe thou shalt him see,
		And ryse up with full victory.
	310	When he hath fulfilled the prophesy,
		Thou shalt him se, full sickerly,
		Within thes days three.
JESUS		Hely, hely, hely, hely;
		My God, my God, I speak to thee.
	315	Hely, lama sabachthany.
		Why hast thou forsaken me?
1ST JEW		A, hark; he cryes upon Hely,
		For to deliver him hastely.
2ND JEW		Abyde and we shall witt in hye,
	320	Whether Hely dare come here, or noe.

---

290. Because your belief (in me) is so true.
293–300. Cf. *John* 19: 26–7.
294. *Ther* introduces a request or command, i.e. 'Look now upon your son'.
302. Death, I call upon you to appear.
313, 315. cf. *Matthew* 27: 46–9.
319. Wait and we shall soon find out.

JESUS		My thirst is sore—MY THURST IS SORE.
2ND JEW		Yea, thou shalt have a drink therfore,
		That thou shalt list to drink no more
		Of all this seven yeare. *Gives Jesus vinegar to drink.*
JESUS	325	Almighty God in majesty,
		To worch thy will I will never wand;
		My spirit I betake to thee;
		Receive it, lord, into thy hand. *He dies.*

CENTURION		Lordings, I say you sickerly,
	330	That we have wrought wilfully;
		For I know, by the prophesy,
		That Gods sonne is he.
		Therfore, sirs, very ferd am I
		To hear this noyce and this crye.
	335	I am ashamëd, verely,
		This uncooth sight to see.
CAIAPHAS		Centurio, as God me speed,
		Peace, and speak not of that dede;
		For of him thou getts no meede—
	340	What needes the so to say.
		But, Longeus, take this spear in hand,
		To pearce his hart, look thou ne wand.
LONGEUS (*to Caiaphas*)		A, lord, I see neither sea nor land
		This seven year, in good fay.

---

321. Cf. *John* 19: 28.

326. I have never flinched from doing your will.

327. Cf. *Luke* 23:46.

342. See to it; don't hesitate to pierce his heart.

343. The name of Longeus shows the dramatist's knowledge of the medieval tradition of St Longinus (from the Greek word for 'lance') – the name given to the soldier who pierced Christ's side. The Venerable Bede, followed later by the *Legenda Aurea*, reported his martyrdom in A.D. 58. The legend can be traced to the *Acts of Pilate*, an apocryphal work dealing with the trial, death and resurrection of Christ and, in some versions, with an additional account of Christ's Descent into Hades. Both traditions—neither earlier than the fourth century in origin—were united in the fifth century and, from the thirteenth century onwards, this joint legend was called the *Gospel of Nicodemus*. The Chester playwright could have known the Longinus-legend from many different vernacular sources.

4TH JEW   345   Take this spear and take good heede;
                  And do as the bishopp thee badd
                  A thing that is great need.
                  To werne, I hould thee wood.
LONGEUS   I will do as you bydd me—
            350   But on your perill it shall be.
                  What I doe, I may not see
                  Wher it be ill or good.

                              He plunges the spear into Jesus.

                  High king of heaven, I call thee here,
                  What I have done, well wott I near;
            355   But on my handes and on my spear
                  Whott water runnes ther throe.
                  And on my eyes some can fall
                  That I may se you, some and all.
                  A, lord, wherever be the wall
            360   That this water came froo?

                              He looks around him and sees Jesus.

                  Alas, alas, and weele away.
                  What dede have I done today.
                  A man I see, sooth to say,
                  I have slayne in this affray.
            365   But this, I hope, very Christ be,
                  That sick and blynd, through his pitty,
                  Hath healed before in this citty,
                  As thou has done me today.

                  Thee will I serve, and with thee be.
            370   For well I leeve, in days three
                  Thou wilt ryse, through thy posty,
                  And save that on thee call.

346–8. And do this necessary thing as the Bishop commands you. If you
refuse, you must be mad.

351–2. I cannot see whether I am doing good or evil.

354. I do not understand clearly what I have done.

357–8. And now some has fallen on my eyes. so that I can see you all.

365. But I guess that this must be the true Christ. . . .

372. And save those who call on you.

JOSEPH OF ARIMATHEA   A, lord God, what harts have ye,
                   To slay this man that I now se?
375   Vengeanc uppon you, witterly,
                   I warrand sone shall fall.
                   Alas, how should I be mery,
                   To se his body, fayr and fre,
                   All totorne upon a tree—
380   That was so principall.

                   Nichodemus, Sir, both you and I,
                   Have cause to worship him, witterly,
                   And his body glorifye—
                   For Gods sonne he is.
385   Therfore goe we, by and bye,
                   And worship him devoutly.
                   For we may therwith, perdy,
                   Win us heaven blisse.

NICODEMUS   Joseph, I leeve this sickerly:
390   That he is Gods sonne Almighty.
                   Goe, aske of Pylate his body,
                   And buryed it shall be.
                   I shall help thee, witterly,
                   To take him downe devoutly,

395   Though Cayphas goe wood therby,
                   And eke also his meny.
JOSEPH   To Pilate, brother, will we gone,
                   You and I togeather alone—
                   To ask his body of our fone,
400   If that it be thy read.
                   A sepulchre I wott ther is one,
                   Well graved in a stonne.
                   He shall be buryed, flesh and bone,
                   His body that is dead.

---

373. Based on *Matthew* 28: 57–9.
380. He who was such a princely leader.
395. Even though Caiaphas should be mad with rage because of it.
401–2. I know where there is a sepulchre, neatly carved out of rock.

They go together to Pilate and Joseph kneels and speaks:

JOSEPH 405 Ben avoose, Sir Pilate in hye
As you sitt in your sea;
A boone graunt, for charity,
To my brother and me.
The body of my lord Messy—
410 That you neiled on a tree—
Graunt us, lord, in suffraynty,
And buryed it shall be.

PILATE Joseph, I tell thee, without nay,
That body thou shalt have today.
415 But let me know, I thee pray,
Whether his lyfe be gone.
Hark, centurio; is Jesus dead?
CENTURION Yea, sir, as ever break I bread,
In him is no lyfe lead,
420 Nor never a whole vayne.
PILATE Joseph, then take him to thee.
Goes, and let him buryed be;
But look thou make no sigaldry,
To rayse him up agayne.

JOSEPH 425 Graunt mercy, Sir of Dignity.
You need not for to warn it me;
For ryse he will, of his posty,
And make us all full fayne.

They now ascend to the Hill of Calvary.
A, sweet Jesu, Jesu, sweet Jesu.
430 That thou must dye, full well thou knewe.
Lord, thou graunt us grace and vertue
To serve the in our lyfe.
That they to thy blisse renew
All that ever to thee be true.
435 For emperour, kinge, knight ne Jew,
With thee they dare not stryve.

405–6. Greetings to you, most exalted Pilate, on your throne.
411. Grant it to us through your sovereign power.
419. There is no life left (*lefde*) in him.
426. There is no point in denying (the body) to me on that score.

NICODEMUS   Sir Josephe, brother, as well I se,
                 This holy prophett is geven to thee;
                 Some worship he shall have of me,
440   That is of might most.
                 For as I leev, by my luteye,
                 Very Gods sonne is he;
                 For very sightës men may se,
                 When that he yeeld the ghost.

445   For the sonne lost his light;
                 Earthquake made men afright;
                 The roch that never had cleft
                 Did cleev then, as men dyd know.
                 Sepulchrs opened in mens sight;
450   Dead men rysen ther by night.
                 I may say he is God Almight,
                 Such signës that can show.

                 Therfor brought here have I
                 And hundreth pownd of spicery:
455   Mirhe, aloes, and many mo—therby
                 To honour him—will I bringe:
                 For to balme his swete body,
                 In sepulchre for to lye,
                 That he may have on me mercy,
460   When he in heaven is kinge.
                                     Amen.

The end of the 16th pageant.   July 27: 1607.

---

440. Who is the most powerful of all.

443-4. Men could see the true signs of this because of the strange spectacles that accompanied his last breath. Cf. *Matthew* 28: 50–5.

X. The Harrowing of Hell

The following version of *The Harrowing of Hell* was presented in the York Cycle
of Plays by *The Sadilleres*, after *The Bocheres* had played the *Mortificacio Christi*
and before *The Carpenteres* pageant of the *Resurrection*. It is the twenty-seventh
pageant and, one can assume, was played against a magnificent representation of
the gates of hell. The text is probably from the mid-fifteenth century; the dialect
is Northern. Stage directions are editorial in origin.
MS: *British Museum, Additional 35290.*

Outside the gates of Hell.

JESUS

  Manne on molde, be meke to me,
  And have thy maker in thi mynde,
  And thynke howe I have tholid for the,
  With pereles paynes for to be pyned.
5 The forward of my Fadir free
  Have I fulfillid, as folke may fynde,
  Therfore aboute nowe woll I bee,
  That I have bought for to unbynde.
  The feende thame wanne with trayne
10 Thurgh frewte of erthely foode,
  I have thame getyn agayne
  Thurgh bying with my bloode.

  And so I schall that steede restore,
  For whilke the feende fell for synne—
15 Thare schalle mankynde wonne evermore,
  In blisse that schall nevere blynne.
  All that in werke my werkemen were
  Owte of thare woo I wol thame wynne,
  And some signe schall I sende before
20 Of grace to garre ther gamys begynne:
  A light I woll thei have

7–8. I shall now set about freeing those I have redeemed.
11–12. I have won them back by paying with my own blood.
 17. All those who acted as my servants, I will carry away from their suffering.
 20–1. (Some sign) of grace to cause their joy to begin. I want them to have a
beam of light.

To schewe thame I schall come sone—
My bodie bidis in grave
Tille alle these dedis be done.

25 My Fadir ordand on this wise,
Aftir his wille, that I schulde wende,
For to fulfille the prophicye,
And, als I spake, my solace to spende.
My frendis, that in me faith affies,
30 Nowe, fro ther fois, I schall thame fende,
And on the thirde day, ryght uprise
And so tille heven I schall assende.
Sithen schall I come agayne
To deme bothe goode and ill—
35 Tille endles joie or peyne—
Thus is my Fadris will.

A light shines into one side of Hell where the patriarchs and prophets are
imprisoned.

ADAM   Mi bretheren, harkens to me here;
            Swilke hope of heele nevere are we hadde—
            Foure thousande and sex hundereth yere
40   Have we bene heere in this stedde.
            Nowe see I signe of solace seere—
            A glorious gleme to make us gladde;
            Wher-fore I hope oure helpe is nere,
            And sone schall sesse oure sorowes sadde.
EVE   45 Adame, my husbande hende,
            This menys solas certayne;

---

28. And to provide the comfort (? release) which I have just spoken about
29. My friends who retain faith in me.
37. The Descent of Christ into Hell is based on the following N.T. passages—
Matthew 27: 52, *Luke* 23: 43 and *I Peter* 3: 18–20—and on the O.T. prophecies
which follow later in the play. The tradition formed part of the *Acts of Pilate*
(see 9: 343 n.) and was a favourite theme for medieval illustration in books, on
church walls and on stained glass windows. Hades or Limbo was clearly conceived as a place or state (neither in Heaven nor Hell) where the souls of pre-
Christian people awaited the Gospel message.
38. We never had such a hope of salvation before.

Such light gune on us lende
In Paradise full playne.

ISAIAH   Adame, we schall wele undirstande;

50   I, Ysaias—as God me kende—
I prechid in Neptalym that lande
And Zabulon, even untill ende.
I spake of folke in mirke walkand
And saide a light schulde on thame lende.

55   This lered I whils I was levand;
Nowe se I God this same hath sende.
This light comes all of Criste—
That seede—to save us nowe;
Thus is my poynte puplisshid.

60   But Symeon, what sais thou?

SIMEON   This, my tale of farleis feele:
For in this temple his frendis me fande;
I hadde delite with hym to dele,
And halsed homely with my hande.

65   I saide; 'Lorde, late thy servaunt lele
Passe nowe in pesse to liffe lastand;
For nowe myselfe has sene thy hele,
Me liste no lengar to liffe in lande.'
This light thou has purveyed

70   To folkes that liffis in leede;
The same that I thame saide,
I see fulfillid in dede.

JOHN BAPTIST   Als voyce criand, to folke I kende
The weyes of Criste, als I wele kanne.

47-8. It was this kind of light that shone brightly on us in the Garden of Eden.

50-4. *Isaiah* 9:1-2.

55-6. I taught this while I was alive on earth and now I see that God has sent it.

61. (I say) this—my account of strange miracles.

65-70. *Luke* 2: 25-33.

68. I do not wish to live any longer.

69-72. You have sent this light ahead of you to men who live on earth; what I told them, I now actually see fulfilled.

73-82. *Mark* 1: 2-11.

75 I baptiste hym with bothe my hande
Even in the floode of flume Jordanne.
The holy goste fro hevene discende,
Als a white dowve doune on hym thanne;
The Fadir voice, my mirthe to mende,
80 Was made to me even als manne.
This is my sone, he saide,
In whome me paies full wele.
His light is on us laide;
He comes oure cares to kele.

MOSES 85 Of that same light lernyng have I.
To me, Moyses, he mustered his myght,
And also unto anodir, Hely,
Wher we were on an hille on hight.
Whyte as snowe was his body,
90 And his face like to the sonne to sight;
No man on molde was so myghty
Grathely to loke agaynste that light.
That same light se I nowe,
Shynyng on us sarteyne;
95 Wherfore trewly I trowe
We schalle sone passe fro payne.

1ST DEVIL Helpe Belsabub, to bynde ther boyes;
Such harrowe was never are herde in helle.

2ND DEVIL Why rooris thou so? Rebalde thou royis?
100 What is betidde, canne thou ought telle?

1ST DEVIL What! Heris thou noght this uggely noyse?
Thes lurdans, that in Lymbo dwelle,
Thei make menyng of many joies,
And musteres grete mirthe thame emell.

79–80. To add to my joy, the Father's voice was made to sound like that of a man.

85–91. A reference to the Transfiguration of Christ. See *Matthew* 17: 1–13, and *Mark* 9: 2–13.

91–2. No human being had the power to gaze directly into that light.

99–100. Why do you shout so? What's the wild din about? Do you know what's happening?

104. And show great and joyful excitement among themselves.

2ND DEVIL	105	Mirthe! Nay, nay, that poynte is paste;
		More hele schall thei nevere have.
1ST DEVIL		Thei crie on Criste full faste,
		And sais he schal thame save.

BEELZEBUB   Ya, if he save thame noght we shall;
110 For they are sperde in speciall space.
Whils I am prince and principall
Schall thei never passe oute of this place.
Call uppe Astrotte and Anaball
To giffe ther counsaille in this case,
115 Bele, Berit, and Belial,
To marre thame that swilke maistries mase.
Say to Satan, oure sire,
And bidde thame bringe also
Lucifer, lovely of lyre.

1ST DEVIL 120 Al redy, lorde, I goo.

JESUS (*outside Hell gates*) *Attollite portas, principes—*
Oppen uppe ye princes of paynes sere,
Et elevamini eternales,
Youre yendles gatis that ye have here.

SATAN 125 What page is there that makes prees,
And callis hym kyng of us in fere?

DAVID (*from within*) I lered levand, withouten lees,
He is a kyng of vertues clere:

---

109. A pun on *save*—'to redeem' or 'to keep secure'.
116. To quell those who show such insubordination.
117. Lucifer (Latin 'light-bearer') was the term used in the Vulgate—and followed by the Authorized Version—to translate *Isaiah* 14: 12. ('How art thou fallen from heaven, O Lucifer, son of the morning!'). On the basis of *Luke* 10:18, St Jerome and the patristic writers used this name as a synonym for the Devil. In Hebrew and Christian tradition Satan (also, the Devil) is the supreme embodiment of evil; as his name implies, he is the adversary who plots against another. In the later books of the O.T. (*Job, Chronicles, Zechariah, Psalm* 119) he is the angelic being hostile to God. For the Fall of the Angels see *Revelation* 12: 7–9.
121–4; 128–32. Cf. *Psalm* 24:7–8.
127. While I was alive I taught quite truly.

A lorde, mekill of myght,
130 And stronge in ilke a stoure;
In batailes ferse to fight
And worthy to wynne honnoure.

SATAN   Honnoure! In the devel way, for what dede?
All erthely men to me are thrall;
135 The lady that calles hym lorde in leede,
Hadde never yitt herberowe, house, ne halle.

1ST DEVIL   Harke, Belsabub; I have grete drede—
For hydously I herde hym calle.

BELIAL   We spere oure gates. All ill mot thou spede.
140 And sette furthe watches on the wall.
And, if he call or crie
To make us more debate,
Lay on hym than hardely,
And garre hym gange his gate.

SATAN   145 Telle me, what boyes dare be so bolde,
For drede to make so mekill draye.

1ST DEVIL   Itt is the Jewe that Judas solde
For to be dede this othir daye.

SATAN   Owe, this tale in tyme is tolde;
150 This traytoure traves us alway—
He schall be here full harde in holde.
Loke that he passe noght, I the praye.

2ND DEVIL   Nay, nay; he will noght wende
Away, or I be ware;
155 He shappis hym for to schende
Alle helle, or he go ferre.

SATAN   Nay, faitour, therof schall he faile;
For alle his fare I hym deffie.
I knowe his trantis fro toppe to taile,

---

133. Honour! In the Devil's name, what has he done to gain honour?
144. And make him go his way. (Colloquially—'Tell him to push off!')
147-8. It is the Jew whom Judas sold only the other day to be put to death.
151. We shall soon lock him up in our jail.
154. If I can avoid it.

160 He levys with gaudis and with gilery:
     Therby he brought oute of oure bale,
     Nowe late, Lazar of Betannye;
     Therfore I gaffe to the Jewes counsaille
     That thei schulde alway garre hym dye.
165 I entered in Judas
     That forwarde to fulfille;
     Therfore his hire he has—
     Allway to wonne here stille.

BEELZEBUB   Sir Sattanne, sen we here the saie
160 That thou and the Jewes wer same assente,
     And wotte he wanne Lazar awaye
     That tille us was tane for to tente;
     Trowe thou, that thou marre hym maye
     To mustir myghtis, what he has mente?
175 If he nowe deprive us of oure praye,
     We will ye witte, whanne thei are went.
SATAN   I bidde you be noght abasshed
     But boldely make youe boune
     With toles that ye on traste—
180 And dynge that dastard doune.

JESUS   *Principes, portas tollite,*
     Undo youre gatis, ye princis of pryde,
     Et introibit rex glorie,
     The kyng of blisse comes in this tyde.
          Enters through the gates of Hell, that open before his voice.
SATAN   185 Owte, harrowe is hee,
     That sais his kyngdome schall be cryed.
DAVID (*from inside*)   That may thou in my Sawter see
     For that poynte of prophicie:

---

160. He lives by cunning and deceit.
164. They should put him to death once and for all (i.e. for all time).
170. That you and the Jews had both agreed on this.
172. Who had been given to us to look after.
173–4. Do you really believe that you can now prevent him from showing the force (of his power)—as he says he will?
178–9. Courageously prepare your well-tried weapons.
187. Cf. *Psalm* 89: 19–23.

I saide that he schuld breke
190 Youre barres and bandis by name,
And on youre werkis take wreke—
Nowe schalle ye see the same.

JESUS This steede schall stonde no lenger stoken;
Opynne uppe and latte my pepul passe.

DEVIL 195 Owte, beholdes oure baill is brokynne,
And brosten are alle oure bandis of bras.
Telle Lucifer, alle is unlokynne.

BEELZEBUB What thanne, is Lymbus lorne; allas.
Garre, Satan, helpe that we wer wroken—
200 This werke is werse thanne evere it was.

SATAN I badde, ye schulde be boune
If he made maistries more—
Do dynge that dastard doune
And sette hym sadde and sore.

BEELZEBUB 205 Ya—sette hym sore; that is sone saide,
But come thi selffe and serve hym soo;
We may not bide his bittir braide,
He wille us marre, and we were moo.

SATAN What, faitours; wherfore are ye ferde?
210 Have ye no force to flitte hym froo?
Belyve loke that my gere by grathed—
Miselffe schall to that gedlyng goo.
Howe, bel amy; a de,   *Satan attacks Jesus*
With al thy booste and bere;
215 And telle to me this tyde,
What maistries makes thou here?

JESUS I make no maistries, but for myne—
Thame wolle I save; I telle the nowe—
Thou hadde no poure thame to pyne,

---

191. And take revenge on you for all your misdeeds.
199. Satan, come and help us to be avenged.
202. If he should attempt any further revolt against authority.
206. But come and try it against him yourself.
208. He'll defeat us, even if our numbers were greater.
211. Quickly see that my weapons are ready.
213. Look out, my beauty! Take this!

220 But as my prisonne for ther prowe.
    Here have thei sojorned, noght as thyne,
    But in thy warde—thou wote wele howe.

SATAN   And what devel haste thou done ay syne
         That never wolde negh thame nere, or nowe?

JESUS 225 Nowe is the tyme certayne
         Mi Fadir ordand be-fore,
         That they schulde passe fro payne,
         And wonne in mirthe ever more.

SATAN   Thy fadir knewe I wele be sight,
    230 He was a write his mette to wynne,
         And Marie, me menys, thi modir hight,
         The uttiremeste ende of all thi kynne.
         Who made the be so mekill of myght?

JESUS   Thou wikid feende, latte be thy dynne.
    235 Mi Fadir wonnys in heven on hight,
         With blisse that schall nevere blynne.
         I am his awne sone—
         His forward to fulfille.
         And same ay schall we wonne
    240 And sundir whan we wolle.

SATAN   God sonne! Thanne schulde thou be ful gladde.
         Aftir no catel neyd thowe crave;
         But thou has leved ay like a ladde
         And in sorowe, as a symple knave.

JESUS 245 That was for hartely love I hadde
         Unto mannis soule, it for to save,
         And for to make the mased and madde;
         And by that resoune, thus dewly to have,
         Mi godhede here I hidde

---

220. Except to keep them as my prisoners in order to test them.

222. You are quite familiar with the terms of the agreement.

224. You who never wished to come near them before today.

230-2. He earned his living as a carpenter and, I fancy, your mother was called Mary—and that's as far as your family tree extends.

239-40. And we shall live together for all time and separate whenever we wish to.

248-9. And this is the reason why I concealed my divinity on earth—in order to fulfil (the plan of redemption) at the proper time.

250　In Marie modir myne,
　　　For it schulde noght be kidde,
　　　To the nor to none of thyne.

SATAN　　　A, this wolde I were tolde in ilk a toune.
　　　So, sen thou sais God is thy sire,
255　I schall the prove, be right resoune,
　　　Thou motes his men in to the myre.
　　　To breke his bidding were thei boune,
　　　And, for they did at my desire,
　　　Fro Paradise he putte thame doune
260　In helle here to have ther hyre.
　　　And thy selfe, day and nyght,
　　　Has taught al men emang
　　　To do resoune and right—
　　　And here workis thou all wrang.

JESUS　　265　I wirke noght wrang, that schal thow witte,
　　　If I my men fro woo will wynne.
　　　Mi prophetis playnly prechid it—
　　　All this note that nowe begynne.
　　　Thai saide that I schulde be obitte,
270　To hell that I schulde entre in,
　　　And save my servauntis fro that pitte,
　　　Wher dampned saulis schall sitte for synne.
　　　And ilke trewe prophettis tale
　　　Muste be fulfillid in mee;
275　I have thame bought with bale,
　　　And in blisse schal thei be.

SATAN　　　Nowe, sen the liste allegge the lawes,
　　　Thou schalte be atteynted, or we twynne;
　　　For tho that thou to wittenesse drawes,
280　Full even agaynste the will begynne.

---

258. Because they did so at my request.
264. And by your present conduct you are acting against law and reason.
275. I have redeemed them by my own suffering.
277. Now since you are prepared to cite points of law.
279–80. Even if you produce witnesses, an equal number can be brought against you.

Salamon saide in his sawes
That whoso enteres helle withynne
Shall never come oute—thus clerkis knawes.
And therfore, felowe, leve thi dynne.
285 Job, thi servaunte, also
Thus in his tyme gune telle,
That nowthir frende nor foo
Shulde fynde reles in helle.

JESUS   He saide full soth—that schall thou see—
290 That in helle may be no reles;
But of that place, than preched he,
Where synffull care schall evere encrees.
And in that bale ay schall thou be,
Whare sorowes sere schall never sesse.
295 And, for my folke ther-fro wer free,
Nowe schall thei passe to the place of pees.
Thai were here with my wille,
And so schall thei fourthe wende,
And thiselve schall fulfille
300 Ther wooe withouten ende.

SATAN   Owe, thanne se I howe thou movys emang—
Some mesure with malice to melle—
Sen thou sais all schall noght gang,
But some schalle alway with us dwelle.

JESUS   305 Yaa, witte thou wele; ellis were it wrang—
Als cursed Cayme that slewe Abell,
And all that hastis hem selve to hange
Als Judas and Archedefell,
Datan and Abiron,

281-3. *Proverbs* 2: 18-19.

286. Job also made this point in his day. (Cf. *Job* 10: 20-2, 14:14).

288. Should be able to find a way of escape out of Hell.

295. Because those who belong to me have been released from such suffering.

298-300. By my will they shall depart—but you must endure *their* suffering (instead of them) for ever.

302. By mixing hatred with (apparent) mildness.

307. And all those who rush to hang themselves.

308-9. Examples of famous Suicides. For Achitophel, see 2 *Samuel* 17: 23. For Dathan and Abiram, *Numbers* 15-17.

310 And alle of thare assente:
Als tyrantis everilkone
That me and myne turmente;

And all that liste noght to lere my lawe
That I have lefte in lande nowe newe:
315 That is, my comyng for to knawe,
And to my sacramente pursewe,
Mi dede, my rysing, rede be rawe.
Who will noght trowe thei are noght trewe—
Unto my dome I schall thame drawe,
320 And juge thame worse thanne any Jewe.
And all that likis to leere
My lawe, and leve ther bye,
Shall nevere have harmes heere,
But welthe as is worthy.

SATAN 325 Nowe here my hande, I halde me paied;
This poynte is playnly for oure prowe.
If this be soth that thou hast saide,
                              (*Aside to the audience.*)

We schall have moo thanne we have nowe.
This lawe that thou nowe late has laide
330 I schall lere men noght to allowe;
Iff thei it take, thei be betraied—
For I schall turne thame tyte, I trowe.
I schall walke este and weste,
And garre thame werke wele werre.
JESUS 335 Naye, feende, thou schalt be feste,
That thou schalte flitte not ferre.

---

313. All who do not wish to learn my teaching.
315. That is, to confess to my second coming . . . (and the items of the Creed, that follow).
322. And live according to my law.
324. But prosperity, as is only right and proper.
325. Take my hand (on this bargain)—I'm satisfied.
334. And cause them to live even worse lives (than before).

Satan prepares to attack Jesus.

SATAN   Feste! That were a foule reasoune;
                  Nay, bellamy, thou bus be smytte.

JESUS   Mighill, myne aungell; make the boune
340   And feste yone fende, that he noght flitte.
                  And devyll, I comaunde the go doune,
                  Into thy selle where thou schalte sitte.

The Angel Michael binds Satan as he cries out:

SATAN   Owt! ay! herrowe! helpe Mahounde!
                  Nowe wex I woode oute of my witte.

BEELZEBUB 345   Sattan, this saide we are.
                  Nowe schall thou fele thi fitte.

SATAN   Allas, for dole, and care;
                  I synke in to helle pitte.

He sinks down into the stage.

The prisoners leave Hell and kneel to Jesus as they speak.

ADAM   A, Jesu lorde, mekill is thi myght,
350   That mekis thiselffe in this manere,
                  Us for to helpe, as thou has hight,
                  Whanne both forfette, I and my feere.
                  Here have we levyd, withouten light,
                  Foure thousand and VIC yere;
355   Now se I, be this solempne sight,
                  Howe thy mercy hath made us clene.

EVE   A, lorde, we were worthy
                  Mo turmentis for to taste;
                  But mende us with mercye
360   Als thou of myght is moste.

JOHN BAPTIST   A, lorde I love the inwardly,
                  That me wolde make thi messengere,
                  Thy comyng in erth for to crye,
                  And teche thi faith to folke in feere;

337-8. That were a poor bargain; No, my fine friend; you shall be attacked (by me).

350. You humble yourself in this way to help us.

356. How your mercy has wiped out our debt.

362. Because you decided to make me your messenger.

364. And teach your faith to people who were in fear (of the law of Moses).

365 And, sithen, before the for to dye
And bringe boodworde to thame here,
How thai schulde have thyne helpe in hye:
Nowe se I all thi poyntis appere:
Als David, prophete trewe,
370 Ofte tymes tolde untill us—
Of this comyng he knewe
And saide it schulde be thus.

DAVID Als I have saide, yitt saie I soo,
Ne derelinquas, domine,
375 *Animam meam inferno:*
Leffe noght my saule, lorde, aftir the,
In depe helle where dampned schall goo,
Ne suffre nevere saules fro the be,
The sorowe of thame that wonnes in woo
380 Ay full of filthe, that may repleye.

ADAM We thanke his grete goodnesse—
He fette us fro this place;
Makes joie nowe more and lesse.

ALL We laude God of his grace.

Here they all sing (*the* Te Deum).

JESUS 385 Adame and my frendis in feere,
Fro all youre fooes come fourth with me;
Ye schalle be sette in solas seere,
Where ye schall nevere of sorowes see.
And Mighill, myn aungell clere,
390 Ressayve thes saules all unto the,
And lede thame, als I schall the lere,
To Paradise with playe and plente.
Mi grave I woll go till,
Redy to rise uppe-right;
395 And so I schall fulfille
That I before have highte.

---

368. Now I see all the items of prophecy made clear.
373. As I foretold, even so I have seen it happen. (Cf. *Psalm* 16: 11).
378. Do not allow souls ever to pass from your (protection).
387. You shall share in every comfort.
396. What I have previously promised.

MICHAEL Lord, wende we schall aftir thi sawe—
 To solace sere thai schall be sende;
 But that ther develis no draught us drawe,
400 Lorde, blisse us with thi holy hende.

JESUS Mi blissing have ye, all on rawe;
 I schall be with youe wher ye wende,
 And all that lelly luffes my lawe,
       Gives the sign of benediction.
 Thai schall be blissid withouten ende.

ADAM 405 To the, lorde, be lovyng,
 That us has wonne fro waa;
 For solas will we syng,
 Laus tibi cum gloria. *They end the pageant as they sing.*

FINIS

---

399. So that these devils may not drag us down (to Hell).
405. Lord, let there be praise to you.

XI. Doomsday

The following version of *Doomsday* is the forty-second and last pageant in the *Ludus Coventriae*. It is unfinished, but when it is compared with the three other (and much larger) pageants on the same theme in the York, Chester and Towneley Play Cycles, our version appears much more severely streamlined than any of them and could well have been shorter in conception. (The Chester version gives considerable scope for the use of music; the Towneley version abounds in lively comic invention.) *The Proclamation* of the *Ludus Coventriae* has this to say about *Doomsday*:

<blockquote>

i   *The xl*ᵗⁱ *pagent shal be the last*
And domysday that pagent shal hyth;
Who se that pagent may be agast
To grevyn his lord God, eyther day or nyth.

v   *The erth shal qwake, both breke and brast,*
Beryelys and gravys shul ope ful tyth;
Ded men shul rysyn and that ther in hast
And fast to here answere thei shul hem dyth
Before Godys face.

x   *But prente wyl this in your mende—*
Who so to God hath be unkende
Frenchep ther shal he non fynde

xiii   *Ne ther get he no grace.*

</blockquote>

Dialect and date as before. Stage directions are editorial in origin.
MS: British Museum, Cotton Vespasian D.VIII.

Here begins the Day of Judgement. Jesus descends with Michael and Gabriel the Archangel. Michael speaks.

MICHAEL   *Surgite.* All men aryse—
Venite ad judicium.
For now is sett the Hygh Justyce
And hath assygnyd the day of dom.

---

i. *Doomsday* is given the number '42' in the manuscript, although it is called the 'fortieth pageant' in *The Proclamation*. For a discussion of the lack of correspondence, here and elsewhere in this cycle, see *Ludus Coventriae*, ed. K. S. Block, *E.E.T.S.* 120 (1960), pp. xxvii–xxxv.

  5 Rape yow redyly to this grett assyse,
    Bothe grett and small, all an sum,
    And of your answere yow now avyse,
    What ye shal sey, whan that ye cum
    Yowre answere for to telle.
  10 For whan that God shal yow appose
    Ther is non helpe of no glose:
    The trewth ful trewlye he wyl tose—
    And send yow to hevyn or helle.

GABRIEL   Bothe pope, prynce, and prysste with crowne,
  15 Kynge and caysere and knyhtys kene
    Rapely ye renne your resonys to rowne
    For this shal be the day of tene.
    Nowther pore, ne ryche of grett renowne,
    Ne all the develys in helle that bene,
  20 From this day yow hyde not mowne—
    For all your dedys here, shal be sene
    Opynly in syght.
    Who that is fowndyn in deedly gylte
    He were bettyr to ben hylte:
  25 In hendeles helle he shal be spylte—
    His dedys his deth shal dyght.

*All those who have risen from the earth cry 'ha-a-a, ha-aa-aa'; and those
alive say 'ha-aa-aa', etc.*

ALL THE RISEN Ha-aa, cleve asundyr ye clowdys of clay,
    Asundyr ye breke, and lete us pas.
    Now may oure songe be, wele-away
  30 That evyr we synnyd in dedly trespas.

ALL THE DEVILS Harrow and owt, what shal we say;
    Harrow; we crye, owt and alas.
    Alas, harrow. Is this that day
    To endles peyne that us must pas.
  35 Alas, harrow, and owt, we crye.

---

 5. Hasten quickly to the Grand Assize.
 12. He will tease out (extract by questions) the exact truth.
 16. Run quickly to whisper (? in confession) your explanations.
 26. His own deeds shall prepare the way for his death.
 33-4. This is the day on which we must go to eternal torment.

RESURRECTED SPIRITS A, mercy lorde, for oure mysdede
       And lett thi mercy sprynge and sprede:
       But, alas, we byden in drede.
       It is to late to aske mercye.

GOD   40 *Venite benedicti*, my bretheryn all,
(*from above*)   *Patris mei*, ye childeryn dere
       Come hedyr to me to myn hygh hall.
       All tho myn suterys and servauntys be,
       All tho fowle wyrmys from yow falle.
   45 With my ryght hand I blysse yow here,
       My blyssynge burnyschith yow as bryght as berall
       As crystall clene it clensyth yow clere—
       All fylth from yow fade.
       Petyr, to hevyn yatys thou wende and goo;
   50 The lokkys thou losyn and hem undo.
       My blyssyd childeryn, thou brynge me to
       Here hertys for to glade.

     Peter, opening the gates of heaven, reveals God on his throne.
PETER   The yatys of hevyn I opyn this tyde.
       Now welcome, dere bretheryn, to hevyn iwys;
   55 Com on and sytt on Goddys ryght syde
       Where myrthe and melody nevyr may mys.

ALL THE SAVED On kne we crepe, we gon, we glyde
       To wurchepp oure lorde that mercyfful is;
       For thorwe his woundys, that be so wyde,
   60 He hath brought us to his blys.
       Holy lorde, we wurcheppe the.

GOD   Welcome ye be in hevyn to sitt;
       Welcum; fro me shul ye nevyr flitt—
       So sekyr of blys ye shul be yitt—
   65 To myrth and joye, welcum ye be.

---

43. All those who are my followers and servants.
50-2. Loosen the locks and open the gates and bring my blessed children to me so that I can cheer their hearts.

DAMNED SOULS   Ha, ha. Mercy, mercy we crye and crave;
A, mercy lorde, for our mysdede,
A, mercy, mercy; we rubbe, we rave.
A, help us, good lord, in this nede.

GOD   70 How wolde ye wrecchis any mercy have?
Why aske ye mercy now in this nede?
What have ye wrought, your sowle to save?
To whom have ye doun any mercyful dede,
Mercy for to wynne?

IST DEVIL 75 Mercy! Nay, nay; they shul have wrake—
And that on here forehed wyttnes I take;
For ther is wretyn, with letteris blake,
Opynly all here synne.

GOD   To hungry and thrusty, that askyd in my name,
80 Mete and drynke wolde ye yeve non;
Of nakyd men had ye no shame,
Ye wold nott vesyte men in no preson.
Ye had no pete on seke nor lame,
Dede of mercy wold ye nevyr don;
85 Unherborwed men ye servyd the same—
To bery the deed pore man, wold ye not gon.
These dedys doth yow spylle;
For youre love was I rent on rode,
And, for youre sake, I shed my blode;
90 Whan I was so mercyfull and so gode,
Why have ye wrought ayens my wylle?

The devils point to different people as they speak.
2ND DEVIL I fynde here wretyn in thin forheed—
Thou wore so stowte and sett in pryde,
Thou woldyst nott yeve a pore man breed
95 But from thi dore thou woldyst hym chyde.

[*A pageant of the Seven Deadly Sins.*]
3RD DEVIL And in thi face, here do I rede,

---

70. Why do you evil doers expect to have mercy?
76. And as evidence (of the vengeance) I point to their foreheads.
85. In the same way you neglected the homeless.
91. Why have you acted contrary to my wish?

That if a thrysty man com any tyde—
For thrust thow he shulde be deed—
Drynk from hym thou woldyst evyr hyde:
100 On covetyse was all thy thought.

IST DEVIL   In wratth thi neybore to bakbyte
Them for to hangere, was thi delyte;
Thou were evyr redy them to endyte.
On the seke man rewyst thou nought.

2ND DEVIL 105 Evyr-mor on envye was all thi mende;
Thou woldyst nevyr vesyte no presoner.
To all thi neyborys thou were unkende;
Thou woldyst nevyr helpe man in daunger.

3RD DEVIL   The synne of slauth thi sowle shal shende;
110 Masse nore mateynes woldyst thou non here;
To bery the deed man thou woldyst not wende.
Therfore thou shalt to endles fere,
To slowth thou were ful prest.

IST DEVIL   Thou haddyst rejoyse in glotonye
115 In dronkesheppe and in rebawdye.
Unherborwyd, with velonye,
Thou puttyst from here rest.

2ND DEVIL   Sybile sclutte, thou ssalte sewe.
All your lyff was leccherous lay;
120 To all your neyborys, ye wore a shrewe;
All your plesauns was leccherous play,
Goddys men ye lovyd but fewe.

98–9. Even if he were about to die of thirst, you always concealed drink from him.

101–2. You amused yourself by slandering your neighbour bitterly in order to anger him.

112–13. Because you were so zealous in pursuit of sloth, you shall go to endless fire.

116–17. Beggars, you wrongfully drove away from their (temporary) beds.

118. You shall follow the slut Sybill (i.e. into Hell). The second devil abuses Sybil because, in medieval legend, she was believed to have foretold the birth of Christ and to have shown the Roman Emperor Octavian a vision of Christ and Mary in the heavens. (Cf. *Stanzaic Life of Christ*, ll. 577–580, 593–644).

        Nakyd men, and febyl of array,
        Ye wolde nott socowre with a lytel drewe,
125   Nott with a thred, the soth to say,
        Whan they askyd in Godys name.

ALL THE DAMNED   A, mercy, lord, mekyl of myght.
        We aske thi mercy and not thi ryght:
        Not after oure dede so us quyth,
130   We have synnyd; we be to blame.

[The catchword at the bottom of the page reads 'DEUS'; but this is the last page of the W quire. The rest is missing.]

123–5. You would not help the naked and the weak (and miserably dressed) not even with a morsel, not even with a rag, if the truth must be told.

129. Do not requite us according to our acts.

Glossary

The Glossary does not pretend to be comprehensive: only those words, and forms of words, are glossed which might present difficulty. Because of the wide variety of texts and linguistic forms, no attempt is made at systematic reconciliation and cross-reference of forms, and the gloss is always to the individual line.

abassed *pp.* terrified, afraid, X 177
abast *pp.* humbled, put out, VIII 285
abite, abye *inf.* pay for, II 323, IV 168
abyde *inf.* wait for, V 116, VI 115
accende *v. subj.* beget, VI 30
accept *adj.* acceptable, I 57
acorded *pa. t.* agreed, VI 76
acquyte *inf.* avoid punishment, VII 243
addull *inf.* addle, VI 386
adeu *interj.* adieu, VI 198
affenden *inf.* offend, III 73
afflyght *adj.* afraid, VII 246
affray *n.* disturbance of the peace, attack, VII 140, IX 364
afray *inf.* disturb, IV 343
aght *pa. t.* owed, II 314
agryse *inf.* horrify, III 56
alde *n.* age, length of years, V 180
aleond *adv.* by land, VI 49
algates *adv.* in any case, always, II 166
allegge *inf.* argue a point, X 277
allowe, alowed *inf.* approve of, admit as valid, X 330; *pp.* praised, II 296
als *conj.* as, such as, X 88
amis, amisse *adv.* wrongly, IV 115, IX 283; **nothing amisse** not at all improperly, IV 338
among *adv.* **ever among** continually, II 391
anely *adv.* especially, solely, V 203
anon *adv.* presently, IV 239
anoy, anoye, anye *n.* injury, vexation, distress, punishment, IV 132, IX 16, 284, etc.
any *inf.* harm, damage, attack, IV 109

apayd *pp.* pacified, IX 211
apertlie *adv.* openly, clearly, IV 354
appech *inf.* hinder, delay, II 95
appose *inf.* accuse, XI 10
are see **or**
aright *adv.* at once, IV 150
armone *n.* music, VI 64
assay *inf.* try, IX 35; *imp.* assert yourself, IX 274
assent (1) *n.* agreement, opinion, VIII 76, X 310; **assent** (2) *v. pres.* agree, IX 90; **alle of thare assente** all who think like them, X 310
atent *n.* intention, purpose, I 82
attende *v. pres.* consider, VII 27
atteynted *pp.* convicted, X 278
augent *adj.* proud, VI 116
aughen, awne *adj.* own, V 200, X 237
avayll *inf.* benefit, profit, VIII 183
avyse, awyse (1) *n.* opinion, VIII 60; (2) *inf.* III 60; *imp.* think about, XI 7
awe *n.* hostility, terror, VII 110
ay *adv.* always, X 243; **for ay** once for all, II 456

badd *pa. t.* commanded, IX 346
baill *n.* jail, stronghold, X 195
bale, bayll(s) *n.* suffering, torment, misfortune, IV 286, V 4, VIII 228: *n. pl.* VIII 125; place of torment, prison, X 161, 293
ball *n.* head (slang) II 388
ban, banys *n.* edict, ban, law, II 59; *n. pl.* VIII 35
band *n.* in captivity, IV 293

bandis *n. pl.* bonds, chains, X 190

barnteame *n. pl.* offspring, IX 11

bassche *v. imp.* alarm, VI 165

bayles *n. pl.* bailiffs, II 405

bayn *n. pl.* bones, mortal remains, II 397

bayne *adj.* ready, obedient, VI 158

bede *v. pres.* offer, VIII 208

bedene *adv.* at once, immediately afterwards, I 17

bedeyn *adv.* together, II 222

beheight, behight *pa. t.* promised, IV 259; *pp.* IX 141

beleyf *n.* assertion, VIII 63

belife, belyfe *adv.* quickly, at once, immediately, II 44, VIII 239

bene, ben *inf.* to be, I 102, III 250; *pres.* XI 19; **bees** is, V 82; **beyn** *pp.* VIII 13

bent *pp.* informed, I 57

bente *pp.* fastened, secured, chained, V 45

berall *n.* beryl, XI 46

bere *n.* clamour, shouting, X 214

betake *inf.* commend, commit, betake oneself, IX 226; *pres.* II 441, IX 327

bett *adj.* better, III 160

beyldys *v. pres.* comforts, protects, VIII 143

beyre *v. pres.* bear, carry, VI 363

bidding *n.* commandment, X 260

bide *inf.* wait, endure, suffer, X 207; **bides** *pres.* X 23; **bidand** *pres. p.* V 4; *pp.* II 61

birth *n.* offspring, child, IX 207

bisse *n. pl.* precious stuff, fine linen, IV 62

blasid *pp.* proclaimed, broadcast, VIII 35

ble *n.* colour, complexion, VI 165

blinne, blyn, blynne *v. pres.* cease, stop, II 324, IV 40, IX 40; *inf.* X 16

blisse *n.* joy, glory, Paradise, IX 292

blist, blyst *adj.* blessed, V 82, 146

bodword *n.* command, V 157

bold *adj.* daring, courageous, frank, VI 199, VIII 234

bone, boone, boyne *n.* request, prayer, II 183, III 87, IX 407

boodword *n.* message, prophecy, X 366

booste *n.* boasting, X 212

boote, bote, boyte *n.* remedy, profit, salvation, I 106, IV 286, IX 195, II 377

bore *n.* anus, crack, II 7.

borwe *v. pres.* protect, save, III 81

boune, bowne *adj.* ready, prepared, IV 165, X 178

boure, *n.* bower, dwelling place, garden V 74

bowndly, *adv.* readily, easily, IV 256

bowrdying *n.* jesting, joke, VIII 117

boyes *n. pl.* ruffians, X 97

braide *n.* attack, onset, X 207

brande, bronde *n.* sword, VI 17, VIII 3

brede *n.* breadth, width, III 156

brede *inf.* breed, allow to grow, V 74; *pres.* III 60; **bredde** *pp.* V 31

brennyng *adj.* burning, I 49

brest *inf.* beat, break open, VII 203

brothel *n.* wretch, VII 145

browes *n. pl.* potage, soup, broth, II 418

browke *v. subj.* enjoy, use, II 186

browth *pp.* brought, VII 85

bryssyng, *n.* bruising, VIII 9

bryth *adj.* bright, I 16

burnyschith *v. pres.* polishes, XI 46

by(e) *inf.* pay for, purchase, VIII 157, 281; *v. pres.* redeem, save, overcome, IV 256, VII 12

byd *v. pres.* request, VIII 157

bydding *n.* request, IV 138

byden *v. pres.* wait, live, XI 38

byldyd *pa.t.* established, III 93

bysmare *n.* filthy one, VII 145

cantelys *n. pl.* tricks, VIII 144

carefull *adj.* sorrowful, VI 406

careyn *n.* carcase, corpse, carrion, III 246

cast *inf.* design, deceive, IX 126; throw a dice, IX 74

catel *n.* wealth, X 242

cater *n.* four (<French), IX 85

cawser *n.* instigator, initiator, VI 403

cawth *pp.* captured, arrested, VII 95

cease *v. imp.* put an end to, IX 209

certifies *v. pres.* confirms, reveals, IV 403

certys *interj.* indeed, VIII 229

charge *inf.*, **charge ut tyll** ordain to the letter, VII 182

chekis *n. pl.* cheeks, II 48

chose *n.* choice, VIII 244

chyde *inf.* scold, curse, XI 95

clere *adj.* shining, X 389

clerkes *n. pl.* scholars, X 283

cleyne *adv.* entirely, VI 353

clowdys *n. pl.* clods, XI 27

cognisaunce, *n.* badge, emblem, title, IX 172

com *pa.t.* came, II 5

compellyd *pp.* controlled, III 224

confounde *pp.* bring to confusion, V 16

conjure *v. pres.* implore, demand, IX 302

consyens *n.* justice, conscience, fairness, VII 198

coolde, colde *adj.* cold, calm, I 71; **colde study** deep thought, VII 224

cordes *v. pres.* agrees with, corresponds, IV 312

cost *n.* region of the land, VI 398

coughte *pp.* caught, obtained, IV 152

counsaille, counsell *n.* advice, plan, secret, II 394, VIII 186, X 114

counsayll *n.* Council, VIII 185

covetyse *n.* covetousness, XI 100

coveyte *v. pres.* long, desire, V 196

cowrte *n.* **men of cowrte** lawyers, justices, VIII 20

coyle *n.* cabbage soup, broth, II 426

F

crave *inf.* demand, beg, X 242; *imp.* II 143

crokyd *adj.* lame, halt, deformed, VIII 94

croppe *n.* throat, VII 130

crowne *n.* tonsure, XI 14

cruel *adj.* unjust, severe, VII 7

crye *inf.* proclaim, X 363

cunnyng *n.* knowledge, I 37

dalyaunse *n.* idle talk, VII 100

daunger *n.* danger, jeopardy, III 77

deare *inf.* injure, harm, IV 223

debate *n.* conversation, parley, X 142

dede *n.* death, X 317

dedis *n. pl.* deeds, acts, VI 412, X 24

deeme, deme *inf.* judge, decide, assume, IV 365, V 67, X 34

defame (*1*) *inf.* pour scorn on, VII 46; (*2*) *n.* disgrace, VII 175

defe *n. pl.* the deaf, VIII 98

degre *n.* **in al degre** in every way, I 61

dele *inf.* share, live, V 232, II 137; **with hym to dele** to have dealings with him, X 63

dere *adv.* dearly, VI 327

dight *pp.* made ready, treated, IV 46, IX 222.

dignytye *n.* rank, status, IV 214

dilfully *adv.* sorrowfully, IX 235

dispyte *n.* injury, act of vengeance, I 45

disteyne *inf.* lose colour, appear unattractive, VII 58

dit *pp.* stopped, II 280

dole, doyl *n.* suffering, sorrow, III 215, X 347

dom *n. pl.* the dumb, VIII 98

dom(e) *n.* judgement, VII 193, X 319

dos *v. pres.* put away, II 161

doted *adj.* mad, raving, IV 235

downryght *adv.* completely, III 102

dowte *inf.* fear, despair, VII 38

dowve *n.* dove, X 88

drawe *inf.* bring (forcibly), drag, X 319; *imp.* pull, IX 145

draye *n.* disturbance, outcry, X 146

dream *inf.* lament, cry out, IX 53

drede *n.* fear, X 137

dreed *v. imp.* fear, IX 278

dresse *inf.* direct, show, VII 116

drewe *n.* morsel, small piece, XI 124

dronkesheppe *n.* drunkenness, XI 115

drynchyng *n.* drowning, III 100.

dure *inf.* endure, V 65

dwell(e), dwellen *inf.* remain, V 65, I 57, X 304

dwill *n.* devil, II 4, VIII 4

dyght *inf.* prepare, make ready, bring about, III 164

dyn *v. imp.* beat, strike, IX 151

dynge down *v. imp.* beat down, strike, X 180

dynne *n.* roaring, idle shouting, X 234, 284

dyspite *n.* scorn, ignoring, I 45

eame *n.* uncle, IX 55

eke *adv.* in addition, IX 396

elde *n.* old age, V 180

elles *adv.* otherwise, X 305

emell *adv.* together, V 110

enderes *adj.* **this enderes night** this last night past, VI 1

endyte *inf.* indict, convict of an offence, XI 103

enforme *v, imp.* explain, III 44

es *n.* ease, VI 191

Evangely *n.* Gospel, IV 355

ever amang *adv.* continually, II 391

everilkone *pron.* every single one, X 311

evyn *adj.* level, steady, on target, III 165

evyn *adv.*, **full evyn** at once, directly, VII 73

expresse *adj.* explicit, direct, clear-cut, IV 372

faitour, fatur(e) *n.* traitor, deceiver, impostor, VIII 37, 311, X 157

fare *n.* fuss and bother, X 158

fast *adv.* quickly, IX 113

faver *n.* features, VI 42

fawcun *n.* shape, figure, VI 37

fawte *n.* fault, VII 22

fay *n.* faith; **by my fay, in good fay** (mild oaths), IX 83, 84

fayles *v. pres.* failest, IX 83

fayn(e) *adj.* glad, IX 21, 428

feared *pa.t.*, terrified, IV 188

fee *n.* property, wealth, II 76, IV 282; **to thy fee** as your payment, IX 66

feele, fele *adj.* many, many times over, IV 31, V 234

feere, fere *n.* company, companion, II 384, husband, III 44; *n. pl.* companions, X 352; **in fere** together, V 204, X 126

feight *inf.* fight, IX 238

fell(e) *adj.* base, cruel, treacherous, wicked, I 59, IV 128

fell *inf.* knock down, end, VIII 233

felle *n.* companion (fellow), VI 319

fende *inf.* protect, X 30

ferd(e) *adj.* afraid, IX 333, X 209

fere *n.* fire, I 80, XI 112

ferly *n.* astonishment, II 156

ferre *adv.* further, X 156; **not ferre** no further, X 336

ferse *adj.* fierce, X 131

feste *adj.* secure, chained, X 335

fete *n.* **on fete** indeed, VI 285

fette *pa.t.* fetched, X 382

feyll *inf.* fall upon, settle upon, VIII 88

feyne *inf.* contrive, VII 56

feynnesse *n.* faintness, III 129

feyrefull *adj.* terrible, awe-inspiring, VI 21

fitte *n.* rage; **fele the fitte** experience madness, X 346

flitt(e), flyt *inf.* go away, depart, drive away, II 303, X 210, XI 63

flume *n.* river, X 76

fois, fone *n. pl.* foes, IV 123, IX 399, X 30

folde *inf.* buckle, bend, III 129

fomen *n. pl.* enemies, VII 264

fonde *inf.* try, endeavour, VII 283

fong(e) *inf.* undertake, begin, III 47, IV 69

foode *n.* foster-child, IX 202

forbot *v. subj.* forbid, II 43

forby *inf.* redeem, atone for, IV 207

force, (*n.***) no force** no matter, II 375

for-fare *inf.* go to destruction, III 226

forfete *n.* sin, wrong-doing, penalty, III 51

for-fetyn *inf.* break the law, transgress, III 237

forgo *inf.* give up, II 193

forme-ffaders *n. pl.* forefathers, V 108

for thy *conj.* because, V 157

forwached *pp.* wearied by watching, VI 242

forward(e) *n.* agreement, VIII 302, IX 5

foull *n.* evil, bad luck, VIII 2

found *pa.t.* tried, succeeded, IX 260

fowndes *v. pres.* advances (to fight), IV 107

fowndyn *pp.* discovered, XI 23

freakes *n. pl.* men, IV 128

free *adj.* noble, V 161, IX 8, 299

frelte *n.* frailty, VII 27

frende *adv.* favourably, III 250

freut, frute *n.* child, offspring, VI 321, IX 197

froo *prep.* from, IX 360

fryght *adj.* loaded, VI 405

fulfill(e), fulfyll *inf.* perfect, achieve, support, carry out, complete, IV 227, VII 179, X 299

full *adj.* full (well-fed), II 310

fullryght *adv.* immediately, VI 342

fun *pp.* found, received, V 153

fure *n.* fury, VI 20

fyled *pp.* defiled, V 171

fynne *n.* fin, IX 150

ga *inf.* go, walk, V 232

game *n.* fun, sport, VII 80

gang *inf.* go, X 303

gars *v.* **it gars**, causes it, II 44

gates, gatys *n. pl.* **other gates** otherwise, II 121; in a different direction, VIII 176

gaudis *n. pl.* tricks, X 160

gedlyng(is) *n.* vagabond, gadabout, fellow, X 212; *n. pl.* II 14

gere *n.* equipment, armour, X 211

ges *n.* guesswork, II 231

geyre *n.* utensil, weapon, VI 390

geyse *n. pl.* geese, II 84

ghost *n.* spirit, IV 391

gibb *inf.* deviate, waver, IV 242

gilery *n.* deceit, X 160

glose *n.* subtle interpretation, evasion, XI 11

goes *v. imp.* go! IX 422

gommon *n.* man, IX 155

gostely *adv.* spiritually, VI 238

grame *n.* wrath, I 42

grame *v. pres.* vex, anger, annoy, III 87, VII 62

granser *n.* grandsire, VIII 12

grathely *adv.* readily, directly, X 92

graved *adj.* cut out, carved, IX 402

grayth *inf.* prepare, make ready, V 19; **grayd** *pa.t.* V 139, 188; **graythed** *pp.* made ready, X 211

grefe, (1**)** *n.* injury, harm, II 67

grefe (2**)** *inf.* grieve, damage, VIII 65

grevance *n.* injury, II 402

groundyd *pp.* based, established, I 1

groved *pa.t.* cultivated, grew, II 199

gryll *inf.* anger, torture, IV 226

gune *v. aux.* **gune telled** told, X 286

gynne *n.* trap, instrument of destruction, III 124

gynne *inf.* bring about, cause, III 235

ha done *interj.* come to the point (give over!), VII 220

halsed *pa.t.* embraced, greeted, X 64

halsyng *n.* salutation, V 147

happ *n.* luck; **in happ** by chance, VII 31

har *interj.* harrow, a cry for and against criminals, VI 324

hard *pa.t.* heard, II 34, IV 347, VI 256; *pp.* VIII 10

hardely *adv.* certainly, vigorously, bravely, II 364, X 143

hardy *adj.* bold, II 12

hareode, harrede *n.* herald, VI 47, 136

harie *n.* vexation, perplexity, VI 168

harlot(tis) *n.* scoundrel, ruffian, rascal, VII 124, X 185; *n. pl.* II 22

harmes *n. pl.* wrongs, misfortunes, X 323

harrowe *n.* outcry, X 98

hartely *adj.* heartfelt, passionate, X 245

harts *n. pl.* hearts, IX 373

hase *pa.t.* have, IX 98

hastely *adv.* quickly, IX 318

hat *pp.* called, II 15

haunsed, haunshed *pa.t.* advanced, raised, exalted, IV 424; *pp.* IV 252

have *v. pres.* capture, arrest, VIII 227

hayll *adj.* whole, well, VIII 101; **hold the hayll,** put yourself right with us, VIII 222

heale, hele *n.* prosperity, state of health, happiness, virtue, IV 50, 250, 399, V 238, X 67, 106

heavenlye *adj.* heavenly, IV 418

hede *n.* circumspection, attention, VI 142

hedus *adj.* hideous, dangerous, VIII 61

height, hye *n.* haste, **in height (hye)** quickly, promptly, IV 98, 149, VII 210, IX 157, 223, X 367

heighte, het *pp.* promised, IV 157, 282

hekis *n. pl.* loops, II 47

hele see **heale**

Hely *n.* Elias, IX 313

hem *pron.* them, VI 340, VII 9, 122

hende (1) *adj.* gracious, I 142, X 45

hende (2) *n. pl.* hands, X 400

hendeles *adj.* endless, eternal, XI 25

hent *v. pres.* seize, VI 366; *pa.t.* suffered, VIII 100

herberowe *n.* lodging-place, X 136

here *pron.* her, VII 82; their, III 103, 125, XI 78, VII 122, 123

heris *v. pres. sg.* hearest, II 40

hertely, herty *adj.* sincere, III 28, 89

hest *inf.* promise, III 165

het see **heighte**

hethyng *n.* scorn, contempt, scoffing, VIII 119

heven-ryke *n.* Kingdom of Heaven, V 99

hevy *adj.* **hevy hall** heavenly hall(?), III 50

heyde *inf.* hide, III 197

hight *pp.* called, promised, VII 213, VIII 290, X 231, 351

hight *n.* **on hight** on high, X 88

hire, hyre *n.* reward, wage, X 167, 260

hoill *adj.* hollow, II 7

hold(e) *n.* stronghold, prison, VIII 236, X 151

holgh *adj.* hollow, empty (starving), II 310

homely *adv.* meekly, familiarly, X 64

hone *v. pres.* delay, tarry, II 133

hope *v. pres.* believe, expect, suppose, guess, IX 365, X 43

hoven *pp.* raised, IX 258

hy *v. pres.* hasten, rush forward, II 43

hye see **height**

hyghly *adv.* with all my heart, sincerely, VII 280

hyght *pp.* called, promised, I 167, V 12

hylist *adv.* most notably, VI 40

hylte *pp.* hidden, concealed, XI 24

hyte *interj.* hurry up, 'Gee-up', II 55

i *interj.* Ay, ah; **I fend** Eh! You devil! II 38; [This ejaculation has many forms, e.g. 'A', 'E', 'Aa', 'Ee']

ich *adj.* every; **ich a sprote** every sprig (shoot), II 290

iee *interj., n.* yea, yes, assent, VI 32

ilke *adj.* same, IX 147; **in ilka a** in each and every, X 130

incumber *inf.* trouble, disturb, VI 21

indite *inf.* accuse, VII 123

indytars *n. pl.* accusers, VIII 24

intent *n.* understanding, IV 322

inwardlie, inwardly *adv.* in my heart, secretly, sincerely, IV 346, X 361

io furth *interj.* Gee up!, II 25

iwys *adv.* indeed, surely, XI 54

jangles *v. pres.* chatters, interrupts, II 6

jesen *n.* place of confinement, labourbed, VI 220, 287

kele *inf.* to cool; **oure cares to kele** to cool our sufferings (in hell), X 84

kend(e), kent *pa.t.* instructed, taught, II 72, V 14, X 50; *pp.* IV 246

kerne *n.* ruffian, VI 308

kidde *pp.* made known, X 251

kinde *n.* flesh and blood, IV 421

knafe, knave *n.* boy, servant, ordinary soldier, II 383, VIII 148, X 244

knawes *v. pres.* knows, X 283

kneleyge *n.* knowledge, VI 85

kun *inf.* know how to, II 185

kutte *n.* a piece of twig used for drawing lots; **to keep thy kutte,** to know your allotted place in society, VII 151

kyd *pp.* known, VIII 171

kynde *n.* nature, V 21

la *imp.* lay, attack, VIII 190

lad *n.* man, fellow, VIII 149

ladul *n.* ladle, VI 387

lake *n.* lack, absence, VIII 85

lare *n.* instruction, VIII 85

last *inf.* survive, stay put, IX 117, 140

lastand *adj.* everlasting, eternal, X 66

laude *v. pres.* praise, X 384

lay *n.* law, way of life, XI 119

layde *pp.* prepared, V 186

leare *inf.* teach, indicate IV 86

leasings *n. pl.* lies, IX 191

leche *n.* healer, physician, II 83

lee *n.* protection, salvation, IX 193

le(e)de *n. pl.* people, tribe, IX 182; **in leede,** among men, VI 311, X 70

le(e)s *n. pl.* lies, I 93, X 127; **without les,** believe me.

leev, leeve(n) *inf.* believe, IX 263; *pres.*, IX 370, 389, 441

lefe *n.* permission, VIII 184

legiaunce *n.* allegiance, attention(?), IX 216

legys *v. pres.* alleges, quotes, cites, VIII 96

leif *inf.* stay, II 195

leke *n.* leak, II 285

lele *adj.* loyal, faithfull, X 65

lel(l)y *adv.* loyally, truly, V 58, 89, X 403

lende *inf.* arrive, remain, alight, V 16, X 47, 54

lengur *adv.* longer, VI 416

lent *pp.* indulged, VII 84

lente *pp.* bestowed, granted, V 216

lere *inf.* teach, instruct, direct, X 330, 391; **lered** *pa.t.* V 16

lernyng *n.* information, instruction, X 85

lesse *conj.* unless, III 20

leste *adj.* least, VII 11

lesy(n)g *n.* lie, I 92; *n. pl.* VIII 67

lete *inf.* **down lete,** abandon, put away, VII 282

lettyng *n.* hindrance, obstacle, I 124

leve (*1*) *v. pres.* believe, IV 153

leve (*2*) *v. pres.* live, VII 278; **levyd** *pp.* X 243, 353

levyng *n.* way of life, III 30

leyde *n.* person, VIII 40

leyn (*1*) *adj.* thin, II 112

leyn (*2*) *inf.* give, II 115

light(e) *inf.* alight, enter, descend, IV 362, V 175; *pa.t.* IV 419; *pp.* IV 327

lightly *adv.* easily, II 217

liste *v.*, **als hym liste** as it pleased him, V 34

loce *v. imp.* look, IX 250

lofe *v. pres.* praise, V 217

loke *v. imp.* see, VI 325

lokid *adj.* looked for, expected, VI 231

lokyn *pp.* locked up, secured from, V 10

lolle *v. pres.* sing a lullaby, VI 353

lond *n.* lands, VI 266

loos *n.* fame, renown, IV 116

lore *n.* teaching, VII 49

lorne *pp.* lost, X 198

losell *n.* idler, vagabond, VIII 152

losyngere *n.* deceiver, flatterer, VI 382

loth *adj.* loathsome, VIII 126

lovyng *n.* praise, V 235, X 405

lowe *adj.* humble, III 11

lowfes *v. pres.* value, VIII 239

lowt *inf.* do reverence, bow down, II 436

lurdans *n. pl.* idlers, rogues, X 102

lurdeyn *n.* lazy lout, III 183

luteye *n.* loyalty, honour, IX 441

ly(g)ht *inf.* alight, descend, VI 379

lyking(e) *n.* wish, will, IV 22, VI 206

lyne *pp.* lain, VIII 131

lyre *n.* countenance; **lovely of lyre** beautiful, X 119

lysense *n.* permission, VI 102

lyth *pp.* alighted, I 165

lyve *n.* **on lyve** alive, IV 443, IX 441

ma *v. pres.* may, VI 25

ma *inf.* make, V 235; *pres.*

madds *v. pres.* drives mad, IX 194

make *n.* mate, equal, I 33, II 443

makes *v. pres.* **makes distance** causes trouble, IV 284

males *n.* malice, VI 23

malison *n.* curse, II 356

manace, manase *n.* danger, harm, threat, III 33, 137

mare *adv.* more, VIII 150, 298

marre *inf.* prevent, hinder, impair, ruin, X 173; *pres.* IX 218; *pp.* VI 304

mase *v. pres.* does, makes, VIII 195

mased *adj.* bewildered, confused, mad, IX 122

massage *n.* errand, messenger, III 245

mast *adj.* most, V 128

mastres, maistries, mastrys *n. pl.* assertions about sovereignty, acts of insurrection, superior airs, VIII 81, 195, X 202

materes *n. pl.* subjects of importance, V 32

mawmentrye *n.* idols, IV 6

mayn *n.* strength, IX 218

meddes *n.* middle, VI 34

mede *n.* just reward, bribe, gift, II 294, VII 164; *n. pl.* VI 313

meet *v. pres.* dream, IV 382

mefe *v. imp.* excite, VIII 150

meke *adj.* submissive, peace-loving, V 101, X 1

mekill, mekyl, *adj.* much, great, large, II 237, VII 44, X 146

mekis *v. pres.* humble (yourself), X 350

mekyll *adv.* **full mekyll,** excessively, VIII 132

mele, mels *v. pres.* speak, talk, IV 30, VIII 139

melle *inf.* mix, mingle, have intercourse, interfere, VII 70, 133, X 302

mende (1) *n.* mind, thought, II 105

mende (2) *v. imp.* amend, redeem(?), X 359

mene, *inf.* signify, comprehend, VI 1

meneye, meny *n.* following, band of disciples, VIII 251, IX 396

mensk *n.* honour, VIII 175

menyng *n.* intention, purpose, mention, reference, VIII 183, X 103

merk *n.* target, III 153

merr *inf.* mar, injure, terminate, V 39

mervell *n.* wonder, miracle, V 1

mese *v. imp.* soothe, calm, VIII 151

messy *n.* Messiah, IX 409

mesure *n.* moderate behaviour, mildness, X 302

mete *adj.* suitable, fitting, VII 199

mete *inf.* meet, VI 265

meves *v. pres.* suggests, V 72

meyn *inf.* complain, II 113

meyn *adj.* poor, meagre, II 111

meyne *inf.* remember, VI 270

meynes *v. pres.* signifies, V 90

mirhe *n.* myrrh, VI 232, IX 455

mirke *n.* darkness, X 53

mischaunce *n.* misfortune, IV 288

mo(e) *adj. adv.* more, additional, X 358, IV 409; **and many mo** and many other things, IX 455

mode *n.* temper, VI 304

molde *n.* earth, I 11, V 61, X 1

mon *v. pres.* must, IX 58

mone *n.* complaint, VII 268

moote *n.* debate, I 110

moote see **moyte**

mornyng *n.* lamentation, III 142

motes *v. pres.* lead, X 256

moved *pa.t.* acted, V 39

mowne *v. pres.* may, XI 20

moyte, moote *inf.* discuss, take counsell, argue, IV 434, VIII 298

mustered *pa.t.* showed, demonstrated, X 86

mut *v. pres.* must, VII 132

mynde *n.* memory, remembrance, IV 392

myre see **mirhe**

mys *inf.* do without, cease, lack, fail, II 219, XI 56

mys-happe *v. subj.* do wrong, sin, VII 20

mys-levyng *n.* evil way of life, VII 154

mysse *n.* wrong, injury, fault, III 95, V 2

myster *n.* attention, (mental occupation), VIII 193

myth *n.* might, I 26

nar *adv.* nearer, closer, VI 219

nawder, nowther *conj., pron.* neither, II 193, VI 376, X 287

nay *n.* denial; **without nay** no one shall prevent it, IX 413

near *adv.* never, IX 353

nede *adv.* of necessity, II 164

nedefully *adv.* compulsorily, VI 329

neld *n.* needle, **not worth a neld** worthless, II 123

neres *n. pl.* ears, V 212

neven *inf.* mention, name, enumerate, V 13; *imp.* VIII 295

newe *adv.* **nowe newe** very recently, X 314

newys *v. intrans.* **me newys** is renewed for me, II 189

noder see **nawder**

none *n.* noon, IX 168

nose *n.* noise, II 11

note *n.* business, occupation, task, X 268

nought *adv.* not, XI 104

nowther see **nawder**

noye *n.* vexation, injury, IV 97

ny *adv.* near, III 157

nye *inf.* annoy, injure, vex, IV 170

o, *num.* one, I 32; **on and all** one and all, II 439

obitte *adj.* **be obitte** be dead, X 269

omell, emell *prep.* among, V 61, VIII 272

one *adj.* own, VI 201

on-wysely *adv.* foolishly, unwisely, VI 203

on-wyttley *adv.* ignorantly, VI 203

onys *adv.* once, VII 252

opyn *inf.* open, XI 53

or, are *prep. adv.* before, V 113, X 98, 154, 156, 345

ordan *inf.* decree, V 69; **ordand** *pa.t.* X 25; *pp.* appointed, ordained, prepared, II 468

ordenaunce *n.* command, provision, III 316

other *conj.* either, II 62

outcrye *v. subj.* publish abroad, proclaim, VII 238

over *adv.* ever, II 184

paies *v. pres.* it pleases, X 82; **paied** *pp.* X 235

pagent *n.* scene (of a series of plays), I 13

pagond *n.* stage of a pageant, VI 305

pall *n.* piece of fine cloth, IX 62

parte *inf.* share, VIII 272; *pp.* IX 145

parties *n. pl.* countries, VI 252

pas *inf.* go, walk, IV 170, VIII 247, XI 28, 34

past *pa.t.* spent his time, played, IX 119

passe (fra) *inf.* depart from, V 111

pay *inf.* satisfy, VIII 198; **payde** *pp.* 184, VIII 299

pay(e) *n.* pleasure, satisfaction, IV 254, 370; **to thy paye** obedient to thy will, V 221

payn(e) *n.* torture, suffering, IX 199; **this is the dwylls payn** the devil makes him do this, VIII 140

perdy *interj.* with God's help, IX 387

perell *n.* danger, blame, VI 402

pertly *adv.* openly, VIII 247; **pertly stylle in this prese** openly here before this crowd, I 5

peryng *pres.p.* appearing, VI 112

pie *n.* magpie, IV 273

pight *pp.* fastened, IX 154

pinne *n.* nail IX 147

piped *pa.t.* squeaked, II 298

pitte *n.* pit (of hell), X 271

place *n.* the acting arena where plays were performed, IV 412

playne *adv.* distinctly, VI 258

plente *n.* abundance, II 202, X 392

plyth *v. pres.* argue, promise, assure, I 32

podyng *n.* pudding, II 386

pon *n.* pan, head (colloquial), IX 109

poplard, poplart *n.* hypocrite, canter, IV 233, IX 119

posty(e) *n.* power, IV 38, IX 269

poynte *n.* argument, item, X 59, 188

prase see **prayse**

pray(e) *n.* prey, capture, spoil, VII 114, X 175

prayse *inf.* appraise, value, VIII 75, 257

prees, prese *n.* press, throng, crowd, I 5, X 125

present *n.* presence, VIII 271; **in present** before them all, I 148

presses, pressiose *adj.* precious, VI 77, 124

prevyd see **prove**

price *n.* renown, fame, excellence, VIII 54

principall *n.* chief ruler, IX 380

profer *inf.* suggest, VIII 197

prove *inf.* test, try, IV 34; **prevyd** *pp.* VIII 55

provyssion *n.* foresight, protection, VI 237

prow(e) *n.* advantage, II 163, X 326

prycke *n.* a young buck (in his second year), III 156

puplisshed *pp.* proclaimed, made public, X 59

pursewe *inf.* follow, observe, X 316

purvay *inf.* provide for, prepare, V 120; **purveyed** *pp.* X 69

pyne *inf.* torment, torture, IX 29, X 219; *pp.* X 4

pyth, pyght *pp.* pitched, placed, set, I 20, 166

quarell *n.* quarry, II 368

quarte *n.* quiet; **in quarte** in good health, safe and sound, II 369

quest-mangers *n. pl.* inquest holders, jury, VIII 25

quite see **qwyght**

quyth *v. pres.* requite, XI 129

qwelle *inf.* kill, VII 106

qwen(e) *n.* woman, I 109, VII 68

qweth *v. pres.* bequeaths, VII 135

qwyght *inf.* repay, III 133; **quite** *pa.t.* II 315

rafe *v. pres.* rants, raves, II 425

rape *v. imp.* hasten, rush, XI 5

rappis *n. pl.* sharp blows, strokes, VI 18

rave, rawe *inf.* cry out, scream, rant, VI 303, XI 68

raw(e) *n.* **on a raw(e)** in a line, one after the other, VIII 92, X 401

rayd *pp.* arranged, devised, planned, VIII 68

read see **rede**

re(a)de, red(d) *inf.* advise, interpret, suggest, V 122, VIII 123; *pres.* II 257, IV 340, VIII 4, IX 69

rebalde *n. pl.* ribald men, X 199

rebawdye *n.* ribaldry, XI 115

rebell *adj.* rebellious, II 291

rede *n.* counsel, advice, plan, I 135, VI 308, IX 400

rede *v. imp.*, **rede by rawe** follow in detail, X 317

redyly *adv.* promptly, XI 5

reepe *n.* sheaf of corn, II 235

rehearsed *pa.t.* enumerated, repeated, VI 258; *pp.* IV 376

rejoyse *n.* rejoicing, delight, XI 114

rek *v. imp.* care, II 247

relasse *n.* pardon (discharge from punishment), II 407

reme *n.* land, kingdom, VI 396

remeved *pp.* changed into, symbolized, V 49

rent *pp.* torn, XI 88

renew *pres.* rejoin, bring back, IX 433

repleye *inf.* repent, X 380

repreve *n.* reproof, IV 230

reserved *pp.* left over, IX 72

resoune *n.* argument, X 255

rewle *n.* form of correction, VII 227

rews *v. pres.* regret, take pity, IX 180; *pa.t.* XI 104

reybukyng *pres.p.* scolding, scorning, VI 395

reyde see **re(a)de**

reydownded *adj.* renowned, VI 44

reydress *v. subj.* direct, guide, alter, VI 237

reyherssid *pa.t.* repeated, VI 258

reypeyre *inf.* take one's way, return, VI 350

righteously *adv.* legally, IX 282

rightys *n. pl.* laws, VIII 45

rose *inf.* please, II 95

rowe *n.* row, order; **on rowe** in a line III 11

rowte *n.* company, assembly, III 24

royis *v. pres.* shout, X 99

rubbe *v. pres.* wring (hands), XI 68

rustyness *n.* decay, corruption, III 230

ryfe, ryff *adj.* abundant, numerous, frequent, well known, I 86, V 100

ryffen *adj.* torn, ragged, II 141

ryth *adj.* right, fitting, I 18

sa *adv.* so, thus, V 90

sad *adj.* complete, full, heavy, I 4, VIII 194

sadde, sadlie, sadly *adv.* forcefully, completely, seriously, grandly, plainly, strongly, III 191, IV 392, VIII 60, 217, X 204, etc.

saff *conj.* except, I 37

sak *n.* guilt, crime, strife, V 193

sall *v.* shall, V 35; **sulde** *pa.t.* V 31

sande *n.* message, V 218, VI 66, 264

sartyne *adv.* indeed, X 94

saw (1) *inf.* sow (seed), II 124

saw(e) (2) *n.* speech, opinion, instruction, II 68, VIII 90, X 397; *n. pl.* prophecies, sayings, Proverbs, V 117, X 281

sawll *n.* soul, VIII 49

sawter *n.* psalter, X 187

sayll *inf.* attack, III 171

scapethryft *n.* waster, II 385

schapp *n.* shape, created being, VI 263

schende, shende, sheynde *inf.* destroy, VIII 204, X 155, XI 109

schoo *inf.* show, explain, VI 175; **schode** *pa.t.* VI 134

scleppe *inf.* slip, III 36

scowte *n.* spy, prowler, VII 144

sea, see *n.* seat, throne, IV 380, IX 405

seede *n.* seed, offspring, X 58

seere *adj.* bright; **solace seere** bright hope, X 41

sege *n.* seat, throne, V 66

seke *adj.* sick, XI 104; *n.pl.* sick people, XI 83

sekeyr *adv.* securely, safely, III 90

sekir, sekyr *adj.* sure, certain, II 295, VII 76

selle *n.* cell, dungeon, X 342

semely *adj.* beautiful, handsome, IX 234

sen *adv., conj.* afterwards, since, VIII 238, 259, X 169

sere (*1*) *n.* Sir, VII 48; *n.pl.* III 10

sere (*2*) *adj.* various, many, X 122

servand *n.* service, VIII 28

sese *v. imp.* cease from, I 3, III 29, VII 17

sette *v. imp.* attack, X 204, 205

settes *v. pres.* surrounds, engulfs, IX 241

sewe *inf.* follow, XI 118

seyn *pp.* seen, VIII 12, 266

shame *n.* pity, XI 81

shappis *v. pres.* plans, X 155

shete *inf.* shoot, III 160

shoyn *n. pl.* shoes, II 153

shrew, shrewe(s) (*1*) *n.* wild fellow, bad lot, evil doer, VII 153, IX 257, XI 120; *n. pl.* II 327, IV 106

shrew (*2*) *v. pres.* curse, II 341

shroes see **shrew**

shunand *pres.p.* **be shunand,** see that you avoid, VIII 4

shyre *adv.* brightly, clearly, II 317

sicker, sickerlie, sickerly *adv.* truly, most certainly, IV 108, 114, IX 307

sigaldry *n.* sorcery, IX 423

sight *inf.* look upon, X 90

signes *v. pres.* means, portends, signifies, IV 389

sith *conj.* because, IX 171

sithen *adv.* afterwards, V 7, X 33

sitte *inf.* remain, X 272 342

skabbid *adj.* scabby, II 248

skald *v. subj.* burn, VIII 4

skape *inf.* escape, II 313; *subj.* VIII 82; **skapyst** *pres.* III 185

skaunce *n.* joke, jest, II 401

skill *n.* what is reasonable, argument, meaning, plan, II 260, VIII 207

skorne *n.* contempt, mockery, VIII 82

slake *inf.* slacken, subside, III 243, IX 225

slape *adv.* smoothly, II 416

slauth *n.* sloth, XI 109

sleight (*1*) *n.* trick, plot, IX 138; **sleyghtys** *n. pl.* VIII 41

sleight (*2*) *adj.* skilful, IX 130

sloo *inf.* slay, VI 374, 419; **sloys** *pres.* II 373

slyke *adj.* such (a one), V 97

smyte *inf.* strike, beat, IV 180; **smytte** *pp.* X 340

socowre *inf.* help, XI 124

solace, solas *n.* comfort, joy, X 28, 407

sonde *n.* sand, III 84

sonde see **sande**

sonder, sondyr *adv.* **in sonder** separately, in pieces, II 155, III 174

sone *adv.* soon, presently, IX 376, X 22

sore *adj.* painful, IX 321

sote *adj.* sweet, pleasant, I 108

soth *n.* truth, X 327

sothlie *adv.* truly, clearly, IV 313

sownde *n.* swoon, torpor, III 1

space *n.* interval of time, leisure, opportunity, V 9, VII 39, VIII 131

spar see **sperde**

spech *n.* speech, doctrine, VIII 49

spede *v. subj.* prosper; **dwyll you spede** may the devil bring you luck II 4

spende *inf.* provide, X 28

spere *v. imp.* bar, X 139; **sperde, spar** *pp.* imprisoned, barred up, VIII 294, X 110

spoyl *v.* destroy, strip, IX 18

sprede *inf.* spread, broadcast, germinate, grow, flourish, III 151, V 43, XI 37

sprote *n.* sprig, stalk, II 290

sprynge *inf.* grow, XI 37

spyll, spylle(n) *inf.* destroy, III 30, VII 60, VIII 83, XI 87; **spylte** *pp.* XI 25

spyr *inf.* enquire, VIII 168

stak *n.* corn-stack, II 241

stall *n.* stall, appointed place, II 376

sted, stedde, steede *n.* place, grave, VIII 127, X 13, 40

steigh *pa.t.* ascended, IV 420

steven *n.* voice, command, II 175, V 15; **stand unto his steven** obey his voice, V 116

steyre *inf.* come near, approach, VI 391

stifly *adv.* courageously, actively, IV 93

stoken *pp.* shut up, imprisoned, barred, X 193

stondynge *pres.p.* admitting, granting that, VII 168

stonne *n.* rock, IX 402

stotte *n.* mare (whore), VII 144

stoure *n.* fight, attack, X 130

stow *v. imp.* seize, secure, VII 124

stowte *adj.* stubborn, self-reliant, confident, XI 93

strang *adj.* strong, IV 294

strean *inf.* stretch, IX 140

strokis *n. pl.* blows, VI 379

stryfe, stryff *n.* debate, complaint, I 110, IX 248

sty *n.* path, II 366

styde *n.* place, VI 373

stynt(e) *inf.* stop, put an end to, V 102; *imp.* VIII 2

substaunce *n.* gist, the main part, essence, IV 443

suffer *v. pres.* allow, permit, IX 282

suffraynty *n.* sovereignty, IX 411

sulde see **sall**

suterys *n. pl.* followers, XI 43

swem(e) *n.* grief, pity, IX 10, 50

swe(v)ens *n. pl.* dreams, IV 382

swyme *n.* swoon, II 27

swyth *adv.* quickly, promptly, III 99, 167

sympull *adj.* manifest, obvious, VI 374

syn *conj.* since, II 166

syth *n.* sight; **by open syth** before your eyes, I 28

syyes *n.* the number of a throw at dice, (possibly a '5' or a '6'), IX 95, 99

ta *inf.* take; **I will me ta** I will commit myself, V 231

take *inf.* capture, seize, accept, VIII 187; *imp.* II 358; *subj.* X 351; **taken** *pp.* II 339

takyll *n.* weapon, bow, III 169

talde *pp.* reckoned, counted, V 182, **told** *pp.* VIII 240

tale *n.* narration, statement, X 273

tast *inf.* probe, search thoroughly, VI 422

tayll *n.* narrative (Gospel), VIII 105

tecuns *n. pl.* tokens, recognizable signs, VI 83

teene, ten *n.* vexation, injury, anger, II 21, IV 224, VIII 226, 268

tend *n.* a tithe, II 73

tende *v. pres.* to kindle fire, III 257

tene *n.* punishment, XI 17

tent (1) *n.* attention, heed, I 87, VIII 105; **tent take** to interfere, II 249

tent (2) *adj.* tenth, VIII 274

tent (3) *inf.* to pay attention, VIII 201

tentys *imp.* probe, investigate, VIII 230

teyn see **teene**

than *adv.* then, VIII 21

thar *v. pres.* need, require, II 293

thaym *pron.* them, II 414

the *pron.* those, they, VI 52, IX 268

thenge *n. pl.* things, I 29

ther *pron.* these, X 97

there *adj.* their VI 46

therfore *adv.* for it, IX 322

thew *n.* courteous action, II 185

tho (1) *adv.* then, IV 199; (2) *pron.* those, VII 272

tholid *pp.* suffered, X 3

thorwe *prep.* through, XI 59

thow *conj.* though, VI 20

thrafe *n.* measure of corn = 2 stooks (12 sheaves), II 197

thrall *pp.* subjected, enslaved, X 134

thraw *n.* a little while, II 30

thred *n.* thread, XI 125

thrift *n.* good fortune, prosperity, II 118

throwe *pp.* suffer agony, VII 247

thry *adv.* thrice, IV 171

thryrty *adj.* thirty, VIII 279

thrysty *adj.* thirsty, XI 97

thus-gate *adv.* in this way, V 210

thyng *n.* subject, VIII 91

tide *n.* time, season, XI 97

tille *prep.* to, X 32

time *n.* **at yere time** at the proper season, II 200

to *adj.* two, VII 265

to-dight *pp.* shamefully treated, IX 235

toke, took *pa.t.* gave, IV 75; **toke tent** gave heed, I 87, 92

tokenyng *n.* signification, V 150

toles *n. pl.* tools, weapons, X 179

tome *n.* leisure, VIII 201

toute *n.* tail, backside, II 63

trantis *n. pl.* tricks, X 159

trast *adj.* honest, faithfull, VIII 287

traste *v. pres.* trust, X 179

travell *n.* work, II 152

traves *v. pres.* trouble, X 150

trayne *n.* trickery, X 9

tretable *adj.* amenable, VII 34

trey *n.* three (of a dice), IX 85

trowe *inf.* believe, X 318; *pres.* VI 111, X 95

truage *n.* tribute, VI 50

truly *adv.* exactly; **truly told** exactly counted VIII 240

trussell *n.* bundle, II 170

tryomfande *adj.* triumphant, VI 40

tryomfe *inf.* be treated royally, VI 182

tundyr *n.* kindling wood; **to tundyr** in little pieces, III 176

twin, twyn *inf.* sever, separate, divide in two, II 325; *imp.* IX 304

tyde *n.* time, IX 204

tyme *n.* time; **in tyme** opportunely, X 149

tyne *inf.* lose, VIII 269

tyte *adv.* **on tyte** quickly, II 53, IX 17; sharply, successfully, X 332

tythyngs *n. pl.* tithes, offerings I 54

tytt *adv.* quickly, promptly, VIII 83

uggely *adj.* dreadful, awe-inspiring, X 101

uncele *n.* unhappiness, VIII 284

unconand *adj.* ignorant, VIII 1

uncooth *adj.* strange, IX 336

ungayn *n.* inconvenience, II 380

un-herborwed *adj.* without lodging, homeless, XI 85

unhyd *pp.* uncovered, revealed, VII 250

unkende *adj.* unnatural, uncharitable, XI 107

unlykeing *adj.* unfavourable, displeasing, IV 142

unwynly *adv.* unpleasantly, distastefully, VIII 189

upsoght *pp.* searched for, VI 331

unthankys *adv.* involuntarily, II 187

vayne *n.* vein, IX 420

velen *adj.* villainous, VI 304

verament *adv.* truly, indeed, honestly, IV 247, IX 89

veray *n.* truth, IV 243

vere *adj.* exact, VI 171

verely(e) *adv.* truly, most certainly, IV 75, IX 335

verray, verre *adj.* true, I 49; very, VI 22

vestament *n.* robe, IX 94

vesyte *inf.* visit, XI 82

veyis *n. pl.* ways; **in veyis wyde,** round in circles, VI 106

viallis *n. pl.* viols, VI 64

waa *n.* woe, suffering, X 406

wafe *inf.* wander, II 432
waffe *inf.* bear, carry, V 53
wake *inf.* disturb, excite, VIII 189
wakyng *n.* watch, vigil, guard, VI 65
walde *pa.t.* intended, V 94
wall *n.* well, IX 359
wan *pa.t.* earned, II 139
wande *n.* rod, branch, V 74
wanne *pa.t.* captured, X 171
war oute *interj.* look out! II 25
warde *n.* keeping, custody, X 222
ware *n.* cloth, IX 44
warn *inf.* refuse, deny, IX 426
warrand *v. pres.* warrant, guarantee, IX 376
warried, warryed *pp.* cursed, IV 271, 159
wast *adj.* wasteful, V 194
waste *n.* **in waste** idly, for nothing, V 52
wat *n.* person, man, II 14, VIII 10
wate *pa.t.* deceived, VIII 283
wawys *n. pl.* waves, III 230
wayle, weale *n.* prosperity, IV 251, 300
waynis *n. pl.* carts, VI 405
we *interj.* Ah! VIII 184
weale see **wayle**
weddur *adv.* whither, VI 97
weder *n.* weather, II 169
weed *n.* garment, robe, IX 36
weer, were *n.* doubt, IV 443, IX 13; **in were** in jeopardy, VIII 59
welthe *n.* prosperity, X 324
wem *n.* stain, defilement, I 129
wemlesse *adj.* undefiled, chaste, IX 215
wen *n.* doubt, supposition, I 111
wend(e) *inf.* go escape, X 26, 153; *pres.* IX 116
wentte *pp.* turned, adapted, V 222
wenyand *n.* time of the moon's wane (unlucky time); **in the wenyand** bad luck to you, II 226
werd *n.* world, I 10, III 102
were *inf.* defend, IV 222

werethe *adj.* worshipful, honourable, VI 56
wex *v. pres.* grow, X 345
weyn *inf.* think, believe, suppose, II 382
weynd *inf.* go, II 78; *subj.* VIII 69, 165
whantynge *n.* lack, absence, III 145
whaynt *adj.* clever, deceitful, VIII 144
wher *conj.* whether, IX 352
whom *n.* home, VI 180, 237
whott *adj.* hot, IX 356
wight *n.* man, soldier, IV 92
wilde *adj.* animal, self-willed, uncontrolled, IV 299
wille *n.* permission, X 297
wilsom *adj.* self-willed, V 125
win (1) *n.* happiness, bliss, IV 205
win (2) *inf.* win, gain, earn, IX 388
wit(e) *inf.* blame, II 322, VIII 211
with *prep.* towards, IV 421
witt(en) *inf.* know, realize, IX 6, 187
witte *inf.* blame, X 176
witte *n.* mind, X 344
witterlie, witterly *adv.* truly, really, surely, sincerely, wisely, IV 95, 169, VIII 87, IX 382
won *adj.* one, VI 32
wone *n.* abundance, II 116
wond(e) *inf.* hesitate, fear, turn aside, IV 80, 91, IX 342, 326
wondurs *n. pl.* miracles, strange events, VI 414
wone (1) *n.* expectation, custom, dwelling-place (?) IV 125
wone (2) *n.* abundance, II 116
wonne *inf.* dwell, live, V 164, X 15, 168; *pp.* secured, IX 127; **wonnys** *pres.* dwells, resides, X 235
wonnyng *n.* place of abode, residence, palace, IV 265
woo *n.* sorrow, destruction, X 266
wood(e) *adj.* mad, raging, tempestuous, I 71, II 159, VIII 155, IX 348
woolde *n.* ground, earth, III 190

woodlie *adv.* madly, insanely, IV 236

worches *v. pres.* work, IV 53

wore *pa.t.* were, V 125, XI 120

worship (*1*) *inf.* honour, IX 382

worship (*2*) *n.* mark of honour, IX 439

wott(s), wotys *v. pres.* knows, VIII 146, IX 64

wrake *n.* misery, torment, XI 75

wrast *n.* twist, trick, VIII 283

wreak *inf.* avenge, IV 123; **wroken** *pp.* IV 101, 120

wrech, wreke *n.* vengeance, VII 90, X 191

wreth *n.* anger, VII 289

wretyn *pp.* written, XI 77

wreyche *n.* act of infamy, VI 398

write *n.* carpenter, X 230

wroghte see **wrought**

wroken see **wreak**

wroth(e) *adj.* angry, VI 282, IX 21

wrought *pp.* done, acted, VI 203, VII 87, VIII 87, IX 330, XI 72

wurchepp *n.* honour, good reputation, VII 59

wyddurde *adj.* withered, shrinking, VI 362

wyght *adv.* strongly, swiftly, actively, III 162

wynk *v. subj.* close the eyes, II 227

wynne *inf.* gain, save, earn, III 121, X 230, XI 74

wynning *n.* gain, profit, IV 143

wyrke *inf.* wound, injure, VI 375

wytt *n.* thought, opinion, VII 226

yatys *n. pl.* gates, XI 49

yeede *pa.t.* went, IX 183

yeeld *pa.t.* yielded up, IX 444

yendles *adj.* endless, eternal, X 124

yerdys *n. pl.* rods, I 140

yere *n.* year, II 109

ylkone *pron.* each one; **ever ylkone** everyone VIII 53

yordes *n. pl.* gardens, fields, meadows, IV 268

Gramley Library
Salem College
Winston-Salem, NC 27108